Crossing Borders

From Behind Enemy Lines in
Nazi Europe to the
Racial Divides of the American South

John Wilson Spence

a memoir

with George W. Grider Jr.

First Edition, June 2018

paperback ISBN 9780692058176
ebook ISBN 9780692058183

LCCN 2018932243

Published by Art Ink Press

Printed by Village Books in Bellingham, WA

Contents

Prologue

It was the only jump I ever made, and it marked one of my life's most blissful moments. I was suspended in a clear blue sky in the quietest place on earth. The mood was interrupted by a Nazi fighter plane nosing in on me. Instinctively, I grabbed the chute's shroud lines and pulled, accelerating my descent. The plane disappeared.

The ground began to approach very fast. A crowd of twenty-five or thirty Breton farmers were standing in a wide grassy field, waving their hands and scarves. None were in uniform; some wore skirts. I landed in soft soil. Overhead the sky seemed filled with parachutes. Our group had put up fifteen planes and we lost five. Fifty men were shot down on a single raid. I gathered up the billowing white mass of my chute, not wanting Nazi pilots to see it and radio my whereabouts to their ground patrols.

I'd hurt an ankle, but not seriously enough to keep me there. I ran toward the welcoming smiles. About fifty men from my bomber group were scattered about the field, all working to hide their parachutes. I was ringed by faces, but the size of the crowd was too large for anyone to risk an overt act of help; there might be a turncoat among them. Five or six French peasants approached. I gave them my chute and my Mae West life vest and asked them in my broken French to destroy the chute. The men took our parachutes and rolled them up. That was their way of helping us out. They wanted the silk, too, and to keep the Nazis from knowing they had aided the enemy. I could hear vehicles on the nearby roads charging around, and guessed they were Germans trying to round us up. Only the Nazis would have cars. I turned to run in the opposite direction.

"Hey Lieutenant!" Sid's voice rang across the field. "Wait for me." Sid Devers was our flight engineer and turret gunner. I paused to let him catch up with me. Then we hurried toward one of the hedgerows that surround many Breton fields. (These high, thick walls consist of a centuries-long accumulation of rocks and debris, swept by wind against the fences separating the fields from each other. Hedgerows were everywhere in Brittany.) We climbed over one, about six feet high. Once out of sight, Sid and I sat down to look at a small map that was part of my escape kit. It portrayed the whole of France, but contained little detail of our surroundings, thus proving of no immediate help. But as navigator I was well versed in the geography of France. I told Sid, "Here we are. Let's head for Spain." Safety was a few hundred miles to the south.

I was born in the South, the American South that is, twenty-four years earlier, at the start of 1919, in Tennessee. Like most American boys growing up in the immediate aftermath of what was known then as the Great War, I believed that someday it would be my turn—that I, too, would go to war. My father had been wounded in the Philippines as a member of the U.S. Army's Philippine Constabulary Corps, a paramilitary police force whose mission was to pacify the Philippine Islands after the Spanish-American War;[1] he returned home in time to start a family and thus avoided the European crisis. Three generations earlier, men had fought in what was known among my white Southern family as the War Between the States. War—and a man's responsibility to it—was something I grew up with.

Before I was born my father succumbed to the Spanish flu in the pandemic that killed fifty million people. My mother treated me as a privileged male child. She made sure I had every advantage, just as she and my father had. I was spared nothing and protected from much; I grew up coddled and spoiled. My gentle mother and the kind relatives who raised me ceaselessly doted on me, a fatherless child. They allowed me willful infractions that would have made Tom Sawyer envious.

My mother was unsurpassed as a parent and a human being, and I recognize how fortunate I was to have her. But the parental holes became evident. I often wonder what role a living father might have played in my upbringing. Standing in an open field one day when I was ten years old, I watched a barnstormer in a World War I biplane dropping leaflets from the sky, inviting people to enjoy an airplane ride for five dollars. But my mother wouldn't allow it.

I imagine each of the houses I grew up in having a secret room—my father's room, which held many wonders. On its walls must have hung photographs of the Philippine jungles where he had served. In quiet hours there, I might have heard his stories, his cautionary tales, his advice. Without access to that room, that life, I believe I missed critical help in facing the world's lessons.

Yet not having a father allowed me freedoms that other boys my age did not enjoy. I got to test my wings. Is it possible that had I had a father I might have been held back? Or would having a father in my life have spelled the difference between failure and success in some of my life's most important episodes?

Today I wonder how much my actions in war served to improve the nation or the world, and also how much harm I inflicted on the civilian population. The struggle did turn me into a man, and I went on to serve my nation in other ways. I'm struck by the paradox: how participating in the killing of other human beings—because that is what war is—improved my life and ultimately the lives of others.

Part I

Blessings

Chapter One

Father, Mother, and Murfreesboro

My parents, John Wilson Spence (whose name was exactly the same as mine) and Eleanor Bonner, were married on a hot August evening in Memphis, Tennessee, in 1916. They were both thirty, which was a little older than usual for the time, and college-educated: he was a lawyer and she was a teacher at the local college.

My sister Anne was born the following year, also in Memphis, where my father practiced. He had every reason to envision a wonderful life ahead—for him, his wife, their new baby, and the children they expected to follow little Anne. He had a strong sense of humor and a great many friends (men who would take an interest in me as time went on). That "American dream" was not to be for my father. Not for my mother, either.

The son of a farmer, Wilson Wade Spence, my father was born at Chestnut Bluff, in Crockett County, Tennessee, a few miles east of Halls, but he gave his address as Halls during his years at school in Murfreesboro and at the University of Tennessee at Knoxville. He had an older brother, Wilson Wade Spence Jr., and a younger sister, Katie Belle Spence.

John's mother died at or soon after the birth of Katie Belle. I don't know much about his mother. She is buried, along with my grandfather, in the Lebanon Methodist Church cemetery (in Madison County) near the Spence farm. I call it that, but the farm was sold a good many years ago to a family named Cherry.

I know little of Father's life as a young boy. Mother found it difficult to talk about him. His family was reasonably prosperous by Tennessee standards. Grandpa Spence probably made most of his money trading cattle and horses, not from farming; the farm must have served as a depot for stock being held for trade. Uncle Wilson continued that business, and Bill Spence, his eldest son, carried it on. Grandfather sent his two sons to the Mooney School in Murfreesboro, which was in Middle Tennessee. It was a highly regarded school, superior to any school in West Tennessee.[2]

At Mooney, my father excelled in academics and sports. He went on to the University of Tennessee in 1904 and joined the Kappa Sigma fraternity. During his senior year he managed the track team. Following his graduation, in 1908, he enrolled in the UT law school where he received his Bachelor of Law degree in 1912.

My father was on the cutting edge of things. He was alert to the times and opportunities, and he had good connections. He became an officer in the Philippine Constabulary Corps. He spent most of a year in the Philippines, sometimes the only white man at a post. He acquired fluency in Spanish. There were many rebellious Filipinos in the southern part of the country, and I believe he was wounded, but I don't know where or how.

When his engagement with the constabulary ended, Father chose to come home by continuing westward, traveling around the world. He visited China, then sailed through the Suez Canal and across the Mediterranean to Spain. He had the good sense and foresight to bring along an Eastman Kodak camera, though it was huge and weighty and he probably had to carry a ton of film.

Upon returning to the States in 1913, he joined a law practice in Memphis. He partnered with some illustrious fellows, one of whom was John D. Martin, later a federal judge. Another partner was Ike Crabtree, who was very kind to my mother and us kids. Father was also a partner with Billy Kaiser.

He and Kaiser had been classmates at the University of Tennessee. Billy Kaiser came from over the Tennessee-Alabama line, from the same town as Kenneth McKellar. McKellar had come to Memphis in 1892 and was an up-and-coming politician. He was elected to the U.S. House of Representatives in 1911, where he served until his election to the Senate. McKellar served longer in both houses than anyone else in Tennessee history. Billy Kaiser later left the law firm to become president of the Memphis Power & Light Company. My father, then, was running in all the right circles for a man just beginning his life in the twentieth century.

Born in Nashville in 1886 to Anne Burton Bonner and Moses Bonner, my mother, Eleanor Bonner, had grown up in the South at a time of both hardship and great opportunity. Anne was the daughter of John Williams Burton, a Tennessee legislator and judge. John Williams Burton's distinction in public life, apart from his service as a judge, was that he was a member of the Constitutional Convention of 1870 that revised the Tennessee constitution of 1834. They didn't write a very good constitution, and they made it hard to amend. Moses was a physician, and his father was also a doctor. Both father and son, I believe, received their medical education in Philadelphia.

Mother was christened Ella for an aunt, but liked Eleanor better and adopted that name when she was free to do so. She had two siblings who died in infancy, a boy and a girl. Two other younger siblings survived. When my mother was ten, her mother died with the birth of the fifth child, who survived. Their father left the motherless children to the care of his wife's sisters, Ella and Lavinia.

All those sisters, they were tough stuff. Women of that generation, Southern women, had to make it for themselves, chiefly in teaching. They all taught: my mother, sister Anne, and her sister Lavinia. Lavina went on to be a full professor at Hunter College in New York City.

It was her Aunt Lavinia who steered my mother into teaching. Lavinia Murfree Burton—I grew up calling her "Granny" but she was also known as Lavinia, Miss Lavinia, Miss Vinnie, and Miss Burton—achieved distinction as a teacher of deaf children. Around 1900, Granny went to Natchez, Mississippi, to be headmistress of a girls' boarding and day school, Stanton Hall, named for its first owners. When Mother was in her early teens, Granny enrolled her in Stanton Hall.[3]

In childhood, my great-aunt Lavinia had had scarlet fever and she had lost nearly all her hair, so she wore wigs. That might have been a factor in her never marrying. When I knew her in her later years, she did not get out very much, just about once a day. She was totally dependent on others for transportation. My Uncle Jesse, Mother's brother-in-law, often took her for a ride in the afternoon.

I know more about my mother's professional life than about her childhood. After graduating from Stanton Hall, she enrolled in Peabody College in Nashville for a year before moving to Florida around age seventeen or eighteen, where she taught at and was the principal of the high school in Eau Gallie. Teachers at that time were very young and often not well educated, so Mother was unusual in the latter respect.

She stayed abreast of the current thinking in education. In the summer of 1907 she went to the University of Chicago to study in the Laboratory School founded by John Dewey, an educational reformer. The following two summers she went to Columbia University's Teachers College in New York to work directly with Dewey. She was teaching school in Memphis, when, in 1912, she was hired to teach English as part of the first faculty at the new West Tennessee State Normal School.[4]

It was in Memphis that she met my father, probably sometime in 1914, when they both resided in the same two-story apartment building at 1870 Union Avenue. The brevity of their courtship might indicate that they were both old enough to know who they were and whom they liked. There is a family anecdote about their meeting. My father had first met my mother's younger sister Lavinia through a college classmate, Hammond Mynders.[5] John came calling to see Lavinia, but she wasn't there; but Mother was and she and John hit it off. They were married the next year, on August 30, 1916.

In the autumn of 1918, I was six months in my mother's womb. My mother and father and my one-year-old sister were living in an apartment at 1733 Poplar Avenue in Memphis. My mother had become a housewife when she married my father. In those long-ago days of streetcars and gas lamps, that's what women did. So my mother set aside her career while Father was busy building his new law firm. Every morning, he would catch the trolley near his doorstep and ride it to his downtown office. Every night, he would take the trolley home.

The war in Europe was winding down, and the Allies had all but defeated the Central Powers. Father had not served in this war; as a family caretaker he was exempt from the draft. His escape from the ongoing terrors of trench warfare must have been on his mind as he ran his practice. I wonder if he thought at all about the more imminent danger: the influenza pandemic. The Spanish flu claimed far more lives (50 million) than the war (16 million). It was fast and vicious: victims often died within hours. Scores of Memphians were dying each week.

We have treatment now: antibiotics, wonder drugs. But penicillin would not be identified until 1928; the first commercially available antibiotic didn't appear until 1932. People don't think about how much the practice of medicine has changed in the last hundred years, but it has. Young adults were among the hardest hit during the flu pandemic. It's speculated now they died from what's called a cytokine storm—an overreaction of the immune system.

In early October, Father came down with pneumonia, the flu's frequent accomplice. On October 6, Dr. Louis Leroy paid a visit to our home.

Father's condition continued to worsen, and on October 12 he died. My mother was by his side. Father was buried in Memphis's old cemetery, Elmwood.

My mother took her infant daughter and went to live with her younger sister, Anne Bonner Huggins (we kids called her Nannee), in Murfreesboro, in Rutherford County, Tennessee. Murfreesboro, originally called Cannonsburgh, was a tiny village when Revolutionary War hero Captain William Lytle donated sixty acres on which to build the town square, in the early years of the nineteenth century. His only stipulation was that the town be named after his friend Colonel Hardy Murfree, another Revolutionary War hero who had recently died. The town fathers obliged, and in 1811, Murfreesboro came into being. Hardy Murfree had been living in Franklin, Tennessee, having moved from his ancestral home in North Carolina after the war. I don't know when the first Murfrees came to Rutherford County, but it was after 1811. By 1919, a lot of Murfrees lived in Murfreesboro—and still do. Many of my Burton and Murfree ancestors are represented in the cemetery on Vine Street, just south of Main.

Anne and her husband Jesse Huggins had generously invited my mother and my sister to stay at least until I was born, or until Mother was ready to return to Memphis and try to resume her career as a public school teacher. Anne and Jesse were childless themselves. My great aunt, Lavinia Murfree Burton, also lived with them.

I was born in a fire-lit bedroom at 404 East Main Street in the wee hours of the first Sunday of the month, January 5, 1919. I was a healthy baby. Mother knew the nursery rhyme about children born on the seven days of the week, which said "the child who is born on the Sabbath day is bonny and blithe and good and gay." Thus she liked to say I was born on Sunday morning, though it might have been Saturday night. Her uncertainty about the time might also suggest that my birth was a bit hard.

The doctor attending Mother at my birth was Bart White. Mother asked him to be one of my godfathers. My other godfather, "Uncle George," was George Darrow, and he lived on another corner of Main and Highland.[6]

The house where I was born was a fine one. Its design and spaces were conventional for its time; such houses were built all over the South, for families who could afford them. It sat close to the courthouse square and business center of the then-small town. Living on Main Street in a small Southern town meant you were somebody; houses on Main Street were among the more substantial ones. Often, they were the mansions. Ours was not a mansion, but a spacious cottage—a one-story house of seven rooms, a long, wide hall, and front and back porches. It was very old—an antebellum house—to which many changes were made over the years.

The rooms were very large, with ceilings ten to twelve feet high. Transoms over the doors let air flow between rooms and halls. Windows were floor-to-ceiling, and wide, as electric lighting was not dreamed of when these cottages were built. There was no central heat, but rather fireplaces in the three bedrooms and in the living room and parlor. Each room shared a chimney with the next room. At first they were heated with wood; coal came later. Long after the house was built, a basement had to be dug for the coal-fired hot air furnace. It must have been an awful job. It was a very small basement with narrow, steep stairs and very little light. This supplemented rather than replaced the coal-fired grates in each room's fireplace. Later still they burned gas made from coal. Natural gas from the ground came many years after that.

When I was growing up, the kitchen had a coal-fired range. In summertime, as a substitute, we used a coal-oil stove that was supposed to make the cook suffer less from the heat.

Houses built that long ago generally did not have bathrooms. They had "slop jars" and washbasins. In more privileged families like ours, black servants, "colored folk," emptied and removed them. The house at 404 East

Main got indoor, flush plumbing before I was born, when the town of Murfreesboro built a sewer system and a public water supply. The indoor plumbing was installed in a room added to the back of the house. The servants were relegated to an outhouse that sat near the backyard garden; it was cold in winter, and became bad-smelling and fly-filled in summer. I blush today as I recall our treatment of our servants (we had three: a maid, a cook, and a "houseboy"). In many ways we were very kind, in others thoughtless and cruel.

A funny thing about that bathroom of ours in Murfreesboro: the door to it had been in the house before the bathroom was added. It had a glass transom. And while changes were being made in the house, a new set of stairs with a landing was put in at the back of the house. The stair landing passed near that glass transom. Anyone who would, literally, stoop so low as to peer through that glass could see into the bathroom—as I chose to do one day while my sister was in there. She saw me, let out a scream, and I was severely reprimanded.

The front living room was the commonly used room. The parlor was located across the hall from the living room. To us children, the parlor was off limits. You rarely went in there, and when you did, you snuck in. It didn't get much use. In shape it was identical with the living room. From the parlor you went into the formal dining room, and from there, into the breakfast room, then the butler's pantry, and into the kitchen. There were bedrooms behind the living room. Upstairs, the attic had been made to hold two small bedrooms, ice cold in winter, insufferably hot in summer. Anyone condemned to those rooms in summer sometimes chose to take pallets onto the roof of the front porch, after the night air had cooled it a bit.

In the winter, we set up the Christmas tree in the little-used parlor, and the toys and other gifts were placed beneath it. (One Christmas I was given a tiny doghouse with a toy dog inside. The dog had something electric in him, and when someone shouted "Rex!" the little dog would come flying out of his house. Nannee said Jesse was as delighted as I was with that toy and almost wore it out playing with it.)

When the house was first built before the Civil War, East Main would have been a narrow dirt track, probably without sidewalks. By my time it had been expanded into a wide dirt road. I remember the day East Main was paved. It was a very exciting event. A vehicle sprayed hot tar on the gravel, a second vehicle spread more tar and gravel, and then came the steamroller, a high, ponderous, slow-moving monster that thrilled us wide-eyed youngsters.

The house stood next to a yellow-brick, Greek-style church (Central Christian Church, established and built in 1908) that sat on the southeast corner of Main and Maney Avenue.[7] There were big trees in front of our house, right at the street and only a few feet from the red-tiled, wide front porch. Maybe, once, the porch was farther from the street, in the days before sidewalks and the widening and paving of Main Street. A large garden of flowers and vegetables was directly behind the house.

The street behind the house, a short block away, was a gravel road, Vine Street. It was a sort of "colored folks" street, although the town's oldest graveyard, where many of my ancestors are buried, was also on it. Blankenship's Grocery was on the corner of Vine and Maney Avenue, maybe a hundred yards behind the house. I was often sent to the store for an item or two.

One summer night, perhaps about 1924, there was a torchlight parade down Main Street. Hundreds of men on horseback, men under white sheets, rode past. They wore masks over their faces, and funny tall dunce caps on their heads: the Ku Klux Klan. It was a long parade. Nothing was said in my hearing to explain it, and the attitude seemed to be "What an amusing show!" There was no indication of approval or disapproval that I was aware of as a child. I remember us saying it was "good as a circus." The horses moved at a moderate pace, and I loved the clatter of their hooves on the pavement.

The house is gone now, demolished by the folks who occupied the church on the corner. Until I was about nine, we Spences spent summers there, and most Christmases, until the Huggins family moved down the street to a larger house; larger, yes, but new, and not as finely built as the old ante-bellum one that forms my earliest memories. By then, my mother had reestablished herself in Memphis, the city where she had been teaching, and where she knew that with the help of her relatives and friends she could earn a living to raise her two young children.

Chapter Two

Memphis

My mother was a great-hearted, joyful, courageous person. After her husband's death, she was determined to return to teaching so she would not be dependent on others. She had accepted with gratitude the help her younger sister was able to give in Murfreesboro. But in September 1919, when I was less than a year old, she brought our small family back to Memphis, where she began to teach at Crockett High.

My father had left Mother as well-fixed as a young lawyer could. He had put me in his will for $1,500, a lot of money at that time. My sister was in for $4,500. And his law partners offered Mother her choice of one of three single-family houses they had bought with Father as an investment. She chose the one at 1422 Faxon Avenue, a brand-new house in the Crosstown District located on the Faxon streetcar line. She was fortunate to not owe a penny on the house. She may also have received financial help from her brother-in-law, Jesse Huggins, from time to time. My father's friends also proved a big help. Chief among them were Ike Crabtree, Luther Jones, and John Martin.

The superintendent of the Memphis City Schools was Robert Lee (R. L.) Jones. He had been friends with both of my parents, and he saw that Mother got teaching positions as convenient as possible to her home. He was a giant of a man, well over six feet, not fat, slow-speaking, deep-voiced, and often laughing. He smoked a pipe. He came to Memphis from Jasper, Tennessee, a small town on the Alabama line not far west of Chattanooga. He had a wife but no children that I know of. He lived his last years, maybe for a long time, at 1625 Carr, in a two-story brick house.

I lacked the good sense to ever ask exactly why Mother picked the Faxon house. It might have been on account of its location on the streetcar line and near Crockett High, at Poplar and Manassas, where she knew she would be teaching. Faxon Avenue between Watkins and Stonewall was a choice area, though not an exclusive one. Owners of the other houses on Faxon were teachers, a telephone company worker, a Railway Express clerk, and a doctor. We had these fine Italian families on Faxon, as Memphis, as a whole, became home to many people of Italian origin during the considerable migration of Italians to the United States in the 1910s and early Twenties.

We had, of course, black servants. There were Annie Rice and Mercer during my childhood. I remember one maid, Minnie Mae, was with us on into my college years. They were always first-name people, you know—Minnie Mae, Mercer, Annie Rice. That is the way we spoke of them. They were very much respected, but that was just the custom, to use first names.

Mother had to hire maids who were also able to serve as our nurses while we were young. They'd dangle us on their laps, and they'd bathe us and dress us, and hug us and kiss us. I think they liked working for us, for my mother, and in Murfreesboro the same was true. There was a servant in Murfreesboro who stayed with the family, I guess, for forty years.

Housing was tight then, so Mother rented out part of our home to relatives and friends. As a consequence, I had no room of my own and had to sleep sometimes on a rather narrow bed alongside the windows in our dining room. Minnie Mae—the maid who was with us for many years and felt free to speak her mind—complained to Mother once that she did not like to see me sleeping there. "Miz Spence, that bed of Johnny's look like a coolin' board to me. I wish he had a better place." A coolin' board was the place a just-deceased body was laid out in preparation for burial. Mother laughed, of course, but she somehow managed to appease Minnie Mae. I remember after that I had first one and then another of the bedrooms for my own.

Mother's sister-in-law Katie Belle Spence and her husband, Frank Conyers, were her tenants for a time. They were typical 1920s folk, doing a good deal of drinking of bootleg whisky and partying, and running around in Model T and Model A Fords, and later in Chevrolets. Katie Belle was a teacher of home economics, I don't remember where. Katie and Mother drove together to national conventions of the National Education Association a couple of times. I recall Mother being an official delegate for Memphis teachers for one or more of them.

Another boarder at 1422 Faxon was Miss Sue Powers, superintendent of Shelby County schools; she and Eleanor were lifelong friends. "Miss Sue," as my sister Anne and I called her, was, like my mother, a large, in fact a somewhat obese woman. Miss Sue succeeded Miss Mabel Williams—also one of my mother's friends—as county school superintendent and could afford any sort of lodgings she liked, so she evidently enjoyed her friendship with my mother, and liked being around us children. I remember sitting in Miss Sue's large, warm lap and enjoying it. She had a throaty, warm chuckle of a laugh, and we heard it often. She had a certain style about her. She got a big car and employed a Negro man, Simon, to drive her on the circuit of the county schools. Miss Sue was a good politician, and she knew it would impress her teachers and principals to see her arrive on inspections in her big, chauffeur-driven car. This went on for many years.

Houses in that period were built on lots that were not bulldozed. There were no bulldozers, only mule-drawn "scoops," hence there was a minimum of grading. Some houses were built at elevations eight or ten feet above the street level. Our house on Faxon Avenue had been built around 1916. It had three bedrooms, a basement with a furnace that gave central heat, a screened-in back porch for the icebox, and a front porch the width of the house.

There was a small, dark hall with four doors to front and middle bedrooms, the dining room, and the bathroom. The telephone was there also. The kitchen was spacious, with a pantry off it and doors to the cellar, back bedroom, back porch, and the dining room. There was a big attic. There was a servant's house at the back of the lot, though it was not occupied; our servants lived in their own homes. They walked or rode the streetcar to work. Once we had a car, beginning in 1928, we could give them rides.

The outside door to the back porch usually was unlocked to let in the maid, the iceman, and maybe the furnace tender. Access to the basement was quite necessary during the heating season. Coal was put into the basement through a low, ground level window. The furnace was hand-fired—that was my job as soon as I was big enough to do it. (It was Mother's job to fire the furnace before that.) The practical way to get the ashes out was to fill a container and carry it up the steps, cross the few steps of the kitchen floor, then out the back door, and dump them somewhere, maybe into the alley.

Along with the streetcar line, Faxon Avenue had gas streetlights lit in the evenings by hand. I remember an old man in horse and buggy making the rounds. This was the very end of the gaslight era,[8] and it wasn't long before all the streetlights were electric.

My mother taught winter and summer, day school, night school, summer school, striving successfully for her independence, taking little of the help generously given by her sisters and brother-in-law. She would take my sister and me along with her to the night school classes and plop us down in the back of the room. Night school classes in the twenties and thirties were older people, ambitious people. A good many of them were probably first-generation Jews from Eastern Europe. They were good students and they admired my mother.

Mother had begun teaching straight out of Stanton Hall, then taught at Memphis public schools and at West Tennessee State Normal School without ever having a bachelor's degree, although she had taken some college level classes before her marriage. Superintendent Jones promised Mother that if she would get B.S. and M.S. degrees, he would give her a principal's post. So she began making plans to get her degrees, teaching day and night to save money.

In 1927, we moved back to Murfreesboro temporarily and in with the Hugginses so Mother could complete her degrees in one hard slog. Mother commuted by train to Nashville, rising before dawn to get to the railroad station. She spent all day at Peabody College, returning home at night. By 1928, having taken classes for some years, Mother had both a bachelor's and a master's degree, the bachelor's from Middle Tennessee State Teachers College in Murfreesboro, and the master's from Peabody College in Nashville. Her master's thesis was a biography of one of our cousins, Mary Noailles Murfree, a great-granddaughter of Hardy Murfree. An American author of popular regional novels and short stories in the late-19th and early-20th century, she wrote under the pen name Charles Egbert Craddock, and for many years her publishers thought she was a man.[9]

After Mother finished her degrees, we returned to Memphis. Soon, no doubt impressed by Mother's ambition and cosmopolitan connections, Superintendent Jones made her a principal. Her first school was Madison Heights Elementary, a small school by today's standards. Madison Heights was located in an excellent neighborhood, where Stonewall Street takes a dogleg at the corner of Court. It was one of those two-story, eight-room buildings. It housed grades one through eight.

Teachers in those days were mostly women, educated women, with good backgrounds. The women who taught at Madison Heights fell into this demographic: they were mostly young, and all well prepared.[10] Mother held the Madison Heights principalship until enrollment decline forced the school's closing, sometime during the Great Depression. It suffered the fate of other Memphis public schools located in the stable residential neighborhoods:

homeowners' children grew up and left, leaving few youngsters to take their places. When Madison Heights closed, Mother and her teachers were transferred to other schools.

Following Madison Heights, mother was transferred to St. Paul School, so named (to everyone's confusion) not for the apostle Paul but for St. Paul Street, on which the school was located. Mother was the principal from the mid-1930s to 1948. All of the students were white, as Memphis schools in the 1930s were not integrated.

The school had served a well-to-do clientele in its first years. But during the depths of the Depression, the old, early families had left or died, and families with jobless fathers living in rented rooms in big old houses sent their hungry, ill-clad children to St. Paul. Mother worked without pay for an extended period of time. Though President Franklin D. Roosevelt's New Deal included plans for America's schoolchildren to be fed, change came slowly, at least from the viewpoint of the children. St. Paul School saw to it that the needy children attending got food to eat and clothes to wear. My mother remembered for the rest of her life the civic sprit and private generosity of Mrs. Lawrence K. Thompson, who led the effort to feed St. Paul's children. Mrs. Thompson was a Catholic and the wife of a very wealthy stock trader.

In 1948, the city school superintendent, Ernest C. Ball, realized that St. Paul could not remain a school for white children because the neighborhood was changing, and he sent its white faculty, Mother included, to other schools. Mother was transferred to a large white high school in a working-class area; this was Treadwell High, and enrollment was huge, about two thousand, as I recall. Mother was returned to classroom teaching, but she soon chose to retire; she was in her sixties.

Chapter Three

A Classic American Boyhood

In those days Memphis seemed like a wonderfully safe city; and we enjoyed our lives there. My mother would put me on the streetcar during the afternoons to go to the Memphis public library, even at a very early age. I'd ride downtown to the Cossitt Library at Front and Monroe. The building was Romanesque in style, with red brick turrets and gables. I remember the library as a pleasant place with great big airy rooms on the west side, the river side. One was the children's library room. I read a lot in those days. I'm sure my mother had some hand in that.

Radio was just beginning to happen in those days. Tennessee got its first radio station, WNAV, broadcasting from the Knoxville area, in November 1921, but we probably listened to WKN, which broadcast from Memphis beginning in April 1922. One of our neighbors, Herbert Morris, put together a crystal set for us. It used a one-person-at-a-time earphone. I don't recall when we moved up to the fancy cabinet models they had in those days. My mother didn't listen to it much; she was too busy. On occasion we listened to *Amos and Andy*, and *Fibber McGee and Molly*. These were comedies and were pretty imaginative.

Life for me on Faxon Avenue was a classic American boyhood. It was a near-perfect growing-up place. We had sidewalks to run our scooters and tricycles on, and backyards fine for football. One of the great treasures of my boyhood was my mother's gift of an Irish mail.[11] I thought it was the greatest thing that was ever made—the perfect sidewalk vehicle for a small boy. Over the course of several years, I rode up and down the sidewalk, probably covering at least 150 yards. In a generous mood I might have taken a passenger. I would fly up and down Faxon Avenue, turning the corner toward Tutwiler a few times, but mostly terrorizing any pedestrian who happened to be using our street. That Irish mail developed in me some pretty good arm muscles, plus leg flexibility.

It was a blessed time in many ways. Faxon Avenue was a typical middle-class American neighborhood. The surrounding houses were much like ours and the parents in our neighborhood held a range of jobs. Our neighbor Mr. Evans worked for the telephone company. Herbert Morris was a high school teacher at Tech High. Mr. Ragsdale, principal of Humes High, lived catty-corner across Faxon from us. Two elderly single women, Sister Reeder and Sister Mac, lived on the south side of Faxon; one kept house and the other clerked at Levy's, an elegant women's store on Main Street. Dr. Fielder was an MD; in those days doctors weren't the rich guys they are today.

On Saturday afternoons, parents would take us boys to the Loew's Palace movie theater on Union and Monroe just off Main Street. We were permitted to go from the movie down to Walgreen's to have a chocolate malted milkshake. Then my mother would come and get us. We'd pile into her car and be brought back to Faxon Avenue.

I raised pigeons in the backyard and sold the squabs to the Peabody Hotel restaurant. And we played football. The city then and still today has a number of what are called "well-house lots." They look like vacant lots because they are the sites for the brick pillboxes that cover, or once did cover, a well in the city system. They were great playgrounds for us. We had one in the next block to the east. Just behind that was a property with two more well houses, one on either end. We called it the Smith Lumber Company field because it was next door to the Smith Lumber Company. It was as long and wide as a football field, and we used it as such. (Sadly, a number of the boys I played football with were killed in World War II.)

We also played card games, table games. There was a lot of that in the days before television. Parcheesi was a big one. And backgammon. When I was around eight years old, I went to my first movie; Mother selected it. It was *Penrod and Sam*, a silent movie adapted from Booth Tarkington's book *Penrod*, a wholesome story. We went in the evening on the streetcar to the Suzore Theater on the south side of Jackson near Breedlove. It was before we had a car. I remember less about the movie than about getting there. Later, on Saturday afternoons, Mrs. Fiedler would take us to the Loew's Palace in her coupe. That was pleasant.

The Number 16 Faxon Avenue streetcar ran right by our house. The cars were noisy, and they ran frequently. The fare was seven cents. Streetcars were very large and airy and had seats of woven straw. The straw often broke and the stalks stuck in our rears. I loved the streetcars. Boys often chose to ride in the back, seated high up on the backs of the chairs. A childhood friend of my sister Anne's, Jean Kirtley of Murfreesboro, once visited us, and she and Anne slept in the front bedroom. Jean was fascinated by the noise and size of the streetcars. (Streetcar lines were very noisy places when a car rolled by, but residents soon became unaware of the noise.) Jean sat up far into the night, listening and watching for the cars.

Mother took my sister Anne and me to church by streetcar many Sunday mornings. Our family attended the Calvary Episcopalian Church downtown. It was Mother's choice. It may have been because of her admiration for Dr. Charles Blaisdell, rector at Calvary in the 1920s and 1930s. On Sunday afternoons, Mother often rode the streetcar to Elmwood Cemetery to visit Father's grave. She took us children along. She stopped sometimes just outside the cemetery to buy flowers or a wreath for his grave.

As the son of a widow who was trying to make ends meet, I had a nomadic life and a checkered school career. Housing was short in the Twenties, so during our summers in Murfreesboro, my mother was able to rent our three-bedroom bungalow in Memphis for short periods of time. When we returned to Memphis in the fall, we might have to look around for some place to board ourselves for a few days or weeks if the renters were still in the house. In 1925, we boarded in a two-bedroom apartment at the southeast corner of Rozelle Street and Lamar Avenue. The house is gone now. I walked to first grade at the Rozelle School, which still stands today.

I should say here that I had entered Rozelle before my sixth birthday, in September 1924. Then I was skipped two "half-grades"—we had those then—though I don't remember which ones. This placed me about a year and a half ahead of my age group. In retrospect, this may have been a mistake.

Before my mother got her first car in 1928, we got around on foot or were given rides with friends, but most often we used the streetcar in Memphis. Taxi rides were costly and rare, but there were occasions when a taxi was the best way to get somewhere, like the railroad station when we were traveling out of the city. It was exciting to get up early to await the cab, ride through the dark streets, and finally reach the cavernous waiting room of the station.

The three of us rode the train from Memphis to Murfreesboro a good many times in those years, first to Nashville, then on another train thirty miles more to Murfreesboro. Railroad stations then were something to remember. Nashville's Union Station was unlike any other: it sat in a deep and narrow ravine that ran through the heart of downtown Nashville. Access to trains was by the steepest, longest set of steps I ever saw.

We reveled in those train trips. (Even later, when I was covering the state legislature in the 1950s, I continued to enjoy riding the trains to Nashville.) We would take "the Pullman," the car with sleeping berths. Having a sleeping berth on a train was, for Sis and me, about as exotic as life got. Trains were crowded then. Cars and buses had not yet seriously diminished passenger train traffic. There would be a lot of drummers on board, as traveling salesmen were called. (They were supposed to be "drumming up trade.") These were splashily dressed, jolly, outgoing fellows. If they had samples that were suitable, they gave them to all in reach. And there were the Pullman porters, black men in white coats, smiling and quick in their movements. Being a Pullman porter was about as high up as a black man in the South could get. (And it may not have been just in the South.) When I used the men's washroom, I noted the porters cleaning the washbowls after each use; they did it with flourish and very quickly. And they got tips for that. They also brushed coats at every opportunity, and they shined shoes. They were ostentatious, but they were not obsequious.

In the summer of 1926, Mother boarded me with our cousin Will and his wife, whom I called "Miss Debbie," at the Gresham Farm just outside Murfreesboro. The site had been a Civil War battleground—the Battle of Stones River—and its fields were still yielding artifacts, including bullets, belt buckles, and Minié balls (hollow pointed bullets).

The Gresham house was typical of antebellum (that is, built before the Civil War) farmhouses. It was, basically, five rooms: a living room and parlor on opposite sides of the wide front hall; a dining room behind the parlor; and two bedrooms upstairs. The dining room was a step or two down from the parlor and opened onto the rear side porch. The fireplaces were wood fires or sometimes coal. But coal could impart an unpleasant flavor to food so it wasn't used in the kitchen.

Lawn mowers were not a part of housekeeping at the Gresham's. A horse would be brought into the dooryard, the spacious fenced area at the front of the house, to mow the grass. I looked up one morning from the living room to see a horse's head at the window, crunching at the grass. I don't know how the flower beds were protected; perhaps they were not tasty.

There is sadness in my memories of those valiant kin; Southern farmers had the decks stacked against them. Cousin Will was a good farmer, but credit for farmers was not well adapted to their needs, and he was struggling to provide and keep the family farm. The crop-lien system, widely used in the agrarian South from the 1860s to the 1920s, was a way of borrowing against anticipated harvests, as after the war, farmers had no cash. Sherman had burned everything down; Southerners had to rebuild every public and private structure, while simultaneously providing for their living. So they borrowed from local merchants all year, then paid their debts after the harvest had been sold. Unfortunately, some years were "bad"—too little rain or too much rain, for example—and the farmer might be unable to pay what he owed, which meant he'd start the next year even deeper in debt. Furthermore, credit given to farmers was at higher rates than other borrowers—and they were charged more for goods by local merchants—precisely because of the uncertainty of their income. This resulted in a cycle of perpetual servitude to the debt, and was disastrous for small family farmers. The Greshams had been struggling for years.

That fall we were all back on Faxon Avenue. I went to Snowden School in the second grade. I walked to Snowden, about a mile from home. One day, I dawdled on the way home, walking the railroad tracks. I was so late getting home Mother was naturally frightened that something had happened to me, and she punished me. That whipping with a peach tree switch may have been the only one she ever gave me.

I spent my fourth-grade year at the Lions Open Air School. My sister Anne was diagnosed, maybe wrongly, as tubercular. At that time, "open air schools" had become popular. Our neighbor Dr. Fiedler thought Anne might benefit from the school, and I was enrolled along with her as a matter of convenience. Located at Fourth Street and Keel Avenue in old North Memphis, the school was built and supported by the Lions Clubs of Memphis. Students sat in classrooms with windows open. The school furnished one-piece, hooded jackets for the children in cold weather.

Following my year at Lions Open Air, I returned to Snowden. Old-time Memphians may recall an amusing story that members of the Snowden family, being big-hearted, offered the city its property. Somebody on the school board said, "That's nothing but a swamp; we don't want it." But the board went ahead and took it. And Snowden School remains there to this day.

Memphis was full of bayous and creeks in those days. It was natural enough—it's in the lowlands of the Mississippi River—but not many people understood this. Of course, we had floods—there was the 1927 flood, for example, and we didn't have all the levees at that time. In fact, the Army Corps of Engineers would begin building the world's longest system of levees as a result of the Great Mississippi Flood of 1927. The water came right into the city. Street cars couldn't run. Flood waters were blocking Faxon Avenue about one hundred yards west of where we lived. The river spread west for forty miles from Memphis to Crowley's Ridge. You could navigate the entire distance by boat. After the levees were built, Memphis became a walled city. With levees in place, it became necessary to install pumping stations to lift the water inside the city over the levees and into the river.

How Mother managed without a car from 1919 to 1928 I cannot imagine. When she got her first Model A Ford in 1928 it must have been wonderful for her. Our first long ride in Mother's new Model A coupe was to my grandfather Spence's farm home at Chestnut Bluff, Tennessee. (This was not the original house, which had been a pleasant, spacious place, I am told. It burned; I think the replacement was not quite so attractive.) Mother asked Katie to join us for the trip. It was a bright Sunday morning.

Chestnut Bluff, today only a wide place in the road, was a few miles east of Halls, in Lauderdale County. Halls was the post office town, and it was on the railroad. The farm sat on the western edge of Crockett County, about seventy-five or eighty miles north of Memphis.

A branch of the Forked Deer River and a wide bottomland separates Chestnut Bluff and Crockett County. Crockett County was one of the last counties to be formed in Tennessee, about 1873. I have long supposed that Crockett residents decided to separate from Lauderdale County because the county, as it now stands, was isolated from its neighbors by the Forked Deer, and they may have received fewer county services than they thought they should. Crockett is one of the smaller counties in area and population; it is rich agriculturally, though not in other ways.

Transportation was difficult in the 1920s. On the trip all four of us—Mother, Katie Bell, my sister, and I—rode in the little coupe, with me lying crunched up on the ledge behind the only seat in the car. I rode all the way, coming and going, in a prone position, fitting comfortably enough.

The highway, which later became U.S. 51, was brand new then. As fast as the road could be paved, it was. It went all the way to Kentucky, passing through to Millington, Brighton, Covington, Henning, Ripley, Dyersburg—a regular West Tennessee thoroughfare. Much of that highway runs through low ground, or, one might say, a swamp. All the West Tennessee rivers have swampy flatlands, bottomlands around them. The road was so new that much wildlife still populated its edges. Sad to say, the droves of turtles and snakes that came out to bask in the sun that warmed the concrete were crushed to bloody messes.

Another feature of the road, I recall, was a one-lane ribbon of concrete through the low, overflow ground, stretching between Halls, where we left the highway, and Espey Park and Chestnut Bluff a mile or so east. To allow cars to pass, small concrete pads were installed about every quarter mile.

That day was one of only two times I ever saw my Grandfather Spence. He seemed as old as Methuselah. I believe he was in his seventies. He had a long gray beard and a massive head of hair that was a bit unruly. He was deaf.

Deaf people in those days carried an ear trumpet. They stuck it in their ear and told you to talk into the mouthpiece. The trumpets were curved things, about a foot long. The apparatus wasn't very successful. I tried to talk with him, and I suppose we communicated a bit.

I made my next, and final, trip to Chestnut Bluff the following year, to attend Grandfather's funeral. It was held at the Lebanon Methodist Church, a few miles from the family farm. What impressed me, the only thing that I remember of that trip, were the horse and buggies. From the inside of the frame church, one could see the black tops of buggies, the horses standing patiently. There were more horses and buggies than I'd ever seen or would ever see again. The horse-as-transportation age was still very much with rural West Tennessee then. Those little horse-drawn vehicles went all the way into the post–World War II era. In Covington, Tennessee, in 1945, there was a horse lot located just off the square. People were still bringing mules and horses into town. We folks were poor down here. Those damn Yankees kept us that way.

It is not pleasant to record, but Mother inherited nothing from her husband's family when Grandfather Spence died. Years later she commented on it to me, saying that she supposed the Spences were in such poor circumstances—any farm family in the South in the 1920s was struggling to survive—that the others thought of her as better off, having her teaching position in the "big city." Men of my grandfather's generation would not have considered my mother family, either; particularly not one who had only been married to a Spence for two years. (In spite of this, my mother went to a lot of effort to maintain ties with my father's family, so we kids would know our relations.)

Such are the things of which family rifts are made, but Mother was incapable of bitterness; one could experience no more bitter event than to lose one's husband when she was only thirty-two and he had just established himself.

If she was not bitter about that, missing an inheritance wasn't likely to throw her.

I lacked the good sense in those years to realize that Katie Belle Spence Conyers, being my father's sister, was the nearest person on earth to resemble him. I know, from Mother's recollections, that the first John Spence had a great sense of humor and was a laughter-loving person. I think today that her laugh must have sounded like his, that things she would think amusing would have amused him; that some of her gestures, even the sound of her voice, might have echoed his.

Chapter Four

Jesse Huggins and the Bonner Sisters

Along with the school year of 1927–28, my sister Anne and I stayed with the Hugginses in Murfreesboro almost every summer in the 1920s and into the early 1930s. By then I don't think I looked forward to these visits, although I didn't regret them. They were simply inevitable.

Jesse Huggins was a generous man. One Christmas he gave me a bicycle as a reward for changing from left-handed to right-handed.[12] I took the new bike out the front door and, despite the intimidating twenty-eight-inch height, somehow managed to straddle it. I rode uncertainly but joyfully up Main Street.

Jesse Huggins was born in 1865, the last year of the Civil War, on a farm near Murfreesboro. He made money early. The story told is that one day, long before he met my aunt, Jesse and others were idly watching a train come to a stop in the Murfreesboro station and saw ice being unloaded. Knowing of an excellent source of spring water, the young men thought, "Why don't we build an ice house?" In those days, ice and coal businesses were usually paired, both being seasonal, so the horses and men employed in one could be put to work in the other. As it turns out, a company, Christy and Huggins, was formed. Sim Christy ran the coal business, while Jesse and his brother Millus built the ice business; it was located on the south side of the Manchester Road.

Jesse and Millus soon added a soft drink–bottling plant. Back then there were a hundred different brands of soft drinks. "The factory," as we called it, became a bottler of Nehi, Orange Crush, Strawberry Soda, and others. Then there was Coca-Cola. Christy and Huggins were the first franchisers to bottle Coca-Cola in the state of Tennessee. Of course, they were unaware that Coca-Cola would become the premier soft drink and the source of a million-dollar business. Jesse was quite proud that people fed Coca-Cola by the spoonful to the sick, even babies; he believed Coca-Cola helped the ill to get well. (When the formula contained cocaine—prior to 1903—it might well have done so.)

In 1931 Mother began teaching during the summers at New York's Hunter College, where her sister Lavinia was a professor. During these summers Mother lived with Lavinia and her husband, Charles Kenneth Eves (who held a Ph.D. and was a professor at Columbia University). Auntee and Uncle Kenneth lived at 90 Morningside Drive, in a spacious and elegant apartment on Manhattan's Upper West Side. They lived on the fifth floor, and their living room overlooked Morningside Park. Mother taught at Hunter College for about fifteen summers. While she was in New York, my sister and I stayed in Murfreesboro.

Staying there with the Hugginses, our rich cousins, was like stepping into the world of the wealthy: big house, servants, fancy cars, the best of foods. The Hugginses had no children, and I think Uncle Jesse wanted me to think of him as a father. He and I would sleep on the screen porch together in the summer. He'd say "Sleep tight and don't let the bed bugs bite. Now let's race to see who can fall asleep first and whoever falls asleep first will whistle."

We went driving on Sundays as a family; sometimes friends came along, but they traveled with their families. We went in two, three, or four cars, and drove thirty or forty miles up the way—a fashionable pastime in those days. Automobiles were no longer new by then. So you piled in your car and drove up to McMinnville to have your Sunday lunch. Or you might go to Sewanee. It was the thing to do.

We drove in big, lumbering cars: Dodges, Fords, Buicks, and Hupmobiles. Maybe a LaSalle or two. We'd go to Betty's Ford or some other ford on the river, one of several that we went to on Sunday afternoons. You went to the fords because that's where you could drive a car across. A ford was naturally a place where there were shallows and rapids, which made for fun swimming or wading or whatever you did. It was easy access by automobile.

In those days everybody wore wool swimsuits. They itched mightily until you could get in the water and get wet. Once the suits were wet they were okay. We drove out of town in the car, itching, scratching, then dived into the creeks or the river as soon as we got there. The women would dress in the car and get out and go dip their toes in the river.

Later Murfreesboro got a swimming pool. All the Murfreesboro boys went out and got themselves junior lifesaving badges, and I got one too. They took to diving, which I didn't do. I was chicken about diving. The swimming pool was on the Tennessee College campus. Somehow this little bitty women's college—a private school run by Baptists—happened to have the town swimming pool. Later on I'm sure there must have been other pools. We visited the fords on Sundays, but we went to the swimming pool every day, all summer long. Maybe twice a day.

Perhaps because the cottage was so crowded, Jesse bought an almost-new two-story red brick house that year. Located at 915 East Main Street, it was just five blocks east of the old cottage. He bought it from its builder, Fletcher Smotherman. It was to have been Mrs. Smotherman's dream house, but Smotherman suffered a business reversal and had to find a buyer. I think it was a deal quickly done; the Smothermans may never have gotten to live in it. A lot of folks went broke in 1928 and 1929. One might think Jesse did Smotherman a favor to buy the house.

Jesse signed the papers without even consulting Nannee. His first words to her on the matter were, "We've got a new house." My aunt was very pleased. Jesse was a wealthy man, and he gave Nannee free rein to buy furnishings and to decorate the house as she wished. She employed a young interior decorator from Nashville, and she spent a good deal of time and money. I was staying in Murfreesboro—it's important to note I thought of myself as *staying* rather than *living* in Murfreesboro—at the time of the move from 404 to 915 Main.

Jesse's purchase of the Smotherman house was a natural enough decision, given how many people he was hosting. It was a Georgian-style house on a very long lot, set back a hundred feet or so from the north side of East Main. There was a two-car garage with a small storage room and, as was usual by then, a flush toilet for servants. The house had four bedrooms, all upstairs, and a sleeping porch. There were electric fans all over the place. Two baths were located upstairs, and a half-bath downstairs. The half-bath was off a downstairs entry room we called the den.

The attic was used exclusively for storage. One thing stored up there was Jesse's five-gallon jug of moonshine. It sat on the landing of the stairs. Prohibition was the law of the land from 1919 to 1933, but few who wanted liquor failed to get it. My Uncle Jesse, very much a law-abiding man in other respects, tapped his jug at midday every day for a single "medicinal" drink. Before lunch each day he bounded up the stairs, went into the attic, and had his one swig of moonshine. It was as clear as water, and it had the kick of a mule. (Oh yes, we kids took samples, at least once.) When the Eveses, who were fond of a drink or two before dinner, made cocktails, Jesse rarely took one. Nannee wasn't much on alcohol.

In retrospect, the house was flawed in many ways. The spaces were ill-designed and badly connected. The den, though small, contained five doors. One of these doors was the back door and thus was the most used door in the house. To use either the back door or the downstairs bathroom, one had to pass through the den. The bedrooms could become unbearable in the summer. Air conditioning had not arrived in Murfreesboro, or many other places, in 1927. Air conditioning was introduced to the general public in 1925 at the Rivoli

Theater in Times Square, and for many years thereafter, the best place to find respite from summer's heat was at the local cinema. By the 1930s department stores and offices had air conditioning, but as late as 1965 only 10 percent of U.S. homes had it.

Though this was a new house, one old way persisted: the servants used a separate toilet located outside the house. At least it had flush plumbing. The toilet, as new as the house, was attached to the garage, a separate building located some distance away from the house. (In later years, servants at 915 Main were allowed to use the bathrooms in the house.) Jesse and Nannee always had a full-time woman who was both cook and maid and oftentimes a "houseboy," a black part-time servant who did heavy work and was a butler for formal occasions. The cook for many years was named Lucy. I am ashamed not to recall her last name just now, but that makes clear the custom of those years. Lucy was our cook for about forty years, maybe more—an excellent one. She was a lady. She had a husband and at least one child. Her granddaughter later taught with me at Shelby State Community College in the 1970s in Memphis.

The Boy Scouts took me away from Murfreesboro for a time, and even from my mother. It was Mother who got me started in scouting—at the early age of nine. There were no Cub Scouts in 1928, so we young boys accompanied the older fellows until we were old enough to join at the required age of twelve.

We spent one week on the banks of the Caney Fork River west of Manchester, Tennessee. It was a crude camp. We slept under old Army tents, with all four sides open to the weather. We had no beds. They'd pitch a tent and say, "Hey, go grab yourself some brush or something to make yourself a bed." No screens, but they did give us blankets. We swam in the river in those days. We took classes in basket making. At Manchester, I discovered an interest in politics, albeit short-lived: we bigoted Southern boys talked about how we didn't want Al Smith, that Catholic from New York, to win the national election. We were just parroting what we heard adults say, of course; I recall having no interest in the 1932 presidential race between Franklin Roosevelt and Herbert Hoover.

In the summer of 1929, I attended Camp Boxwell, a few miles west of Nashville on the banks of the Harpeth River. Camp Boxwell was not as crude as Manchester. I must have been taken there by the Hugginses. Other campers "like us" were numerous, but so were some "not like us." There were the kids from the State Reformatory. Tough kids. I don't think there was hostility between the two groups or classes, but we were a bit afraid of them. I wonder whose idea it was to try to mix Main Street kids with the back street kids. We did not mix much.

It was here at Boxwell that I first remember learning to use the buddy system when swimming. Swimming was the main attraction at both those scout camps. I got to be a fine swimmer, and maybe did some boxing. I continued to pursue boxing back home in Memphis. The YMCA ran a "Man for Boy" program, and a Memphis dentist, Dr. Wesley McKinney, paid $8 a year for a fatherless boy's membership at the Y. I was his beneficiary for three years.

Chapter Five

Communities

When I was a boy it seemed like I was related to half of Murfreesboro. The backyard at 915 Main stretched all the way to Lytle Street, and we kids were told the Lytles were somehow kin to us. We called the novelist Andrew Lytle "Cousin Andruh." Not Andrew. Upon meeting someone new, Southerners still look to determine kin relationships first.

My mother was a very friendly, social woman. She did a lot to see that we children were introduced to everybody we ought to know and learn what we needed to get along in polite society. Mother began taking me and my sister Anne to ballroom dancing classes sponsored by the Memphis Park Commission when I was about thirteen, in part to accommodate my growing interest in girls. Large numbers of boys and girls filled a Park Commission hall. The dancing teacher was an older woman. You danced by the numbers, left foot, right foot, one two three four. So we learned to dance. My father's prominence and my mother's care saw to it that I was invited to all the debutante balls by the late 1930s, although I was rather impecunious, being a woman schoolteacher's son. My mother made sure I had a tuxedo, and I inherited tails from my father, which I wore once or twice when I was grown. It was quite an event to put them on.

When I finally became an official Boy Scout. I became the troop scribe. I believe the job had to do with taking attendance and making reports. We held contests in those days, competition between troops. Our lives were very healthy and fairly physical. Various skills were required: signaling in semaphore, signaling in Morse code. There was knot tying, there was rope climbing, there was fire building. I loved Scouting as it was then. I memorized stuff, studied and won merit badges, went from Tenderfoot to Second Class, First Class, Star, Life, and finally to Eagle Scout with twenty-one merit badges. I attained the rank of Eagle Scout when I was fourteen. I stayed in scouting until I left Memphis for Sewanee Military Academy.

In the fall of 1932, I entered Central High School as a tenth-grader. Central was a fine public school, dating back to about 1908, and the first high school in the Memphis system. It had a large enrollment. It also had fine teachers, mostly women with degrees from Vanderbilt University or Peabody College, both in Nashville. They were all spinster ladies. We had JROTC. Uniforms were a savings on store-bought clothes in the Depression years. We were tickled to have some new clothes to wear, especially GI uniforms.

Tom White and Charlie Freeburg and Bailey Brown and George Keeler were my classmates. In those days, we kept mostly to our own social strata and our own race. We barely acknowledged the existence of two senior highs for blacks: Booker T. Washington and Manassas. I remember I had a date with a Catholic girl once, and it made conversation; I didn't have anything to do with Catholics or Jews until high school. We had a lot of Jewish students. They were smart. Good students.

It wasn't that I hadn't been exposed to them. Jewish people lived on Faxon Avenue; the Italians who lived on Faxon were almost certainly Catholics. They were the Barassos and the Barzizzas. They were in business and successful. I don't recall there was any feeling toward or against them. Our parents didn't see them socially, though, unless it had something to do with the neighborhood.

One spring afternoon, I came cheerily home from school. There I found a grizzled old man in a khaki uniform sitting in our living room talking with my mother, who must have invited him. He was Rutherford Cravens— Colonel Cravens to the cadets at Sewanee Military Academy (SMA), a private boarding school in Tennessee; he had come to talk to Mother about my attendance. Though it was the depths of the Depression, our finances were better than most; Mother had not encroached on the $1,500 trust fund from life insurance my father had left me. By the time I arrived home, Col. Cravens had convinced her that SMA was the place for me. Mother signed me up to go in September as an eleventh grader. I had never heard of the place, but it sounded pretty attractive. Girls liked guys in uniforms, though SMA, need I say, enrolled only boys. And I would have men for teachers. Men teachers were almost nonexistent in public schools.

I never bothered to ask about the interview, how it came about. Did Mother inquire herself, or did SMA canvas homes for enrollees? I was not making the most of my potential as a fourteen-year-old at Central High nor was I meeting Mother's expectations of me as a scholar, although I was excelling in scouting.

Sewanee was a tiny school. There were fewer than one hundred cadets in the student body. We came from all over the South and even from the East, as well as the Louisville-Cincinnati area. The student who had traveled farthest, as I recall, was a fellow from New Jersey.

Sewanee Military Academy was located in Sewanee, Tennessee, on the western edge of the Cumberland Plateau. How closely SMA was connected administratively to the University of the South, located in the same town, I don't know.[13] Physically, it could not have been closer: a quarter- or half-mile from the university campus. SMA cadets wore a handsome uniform; I'd call it Confederate gray, not that we were encouraged to associate ourselves with the Confederacy. We had a single large building, a four-story concrete-and-stone structure in keeping with the buildings of the university. The whole of the academy, except for the athletic buildings and fraternity houses, was contained in this building, called Quintard Hall, and it housed all but a handful of us.

Most of us were in high school—only a few students attended in grades seven and eight. More cadets were enrolled in the higher grades than the lower. Keep in mind this was in the very depths of the Great Depression. Few parents could afford the cost, and so they delayed sending their sons. So it was truly a college preparatory school. All the teachers were men and they wore uniforms and called themselves by various officer ranks.

Sewanee had good teachers. We who made good grades were rewarded with the privilege of strutting off one night a week to the university's student union to see a movie. I much enjoyed watching actors like Greta Garbo in *Anna Karenina* and William Powell and Myrna Loy in *The Thin Man*. SMA was very much an Episcopalian school; every week we were marched to the university chapel for Sunday services.

The school had three or four fraternities, each with a little farmhouse on the west edge of the parade ground-football field. I got bids from more than one, and decided on Tau Delta Phi. The fraternity made little impression on me. The main benefit, if benefit it was, was that once or twice I got to attend Tau Delta Phi's crap games at the Peabody Hotel, in Memphis.

I was well liked by my classmates. I acquired the nicknames Sunshine and Happy John. And while the sobriquets were left behind at SMA, the memory of them has stayed with me all these years.

During this time, I was troubled by a bad case of acne. Mother paid for me to make weekly, or maybe monthly, trips from Sewanee to Chattanooga for treatments: X-ray treatments. Doctors didn't know better then. The trips were made very early on Saturday mornings. Greyhound buses hadn't gotten to Sewanee by 1933. The commercial vehicles that traveled in that day were old limousines: Packard, Lincoln, Cadillac, Duesenberg.

The summer of 1934, I met the legendary Boss Crump. I was thinking it would be nice to go to West Point or Annapolis. My mother, then a high school principal with sufficient contacts to be given an audience, took me downtown to his office. He was our Congressional representative at the time, serving the second of his two terms. Mother asked him, "Mr. Crump, please, will you see to it that John gets an appointment to one of the academies?" He got me a second alternate appointment, but it never materialized.

Sewanee had an excellent athletic facility, with indoor swimming pool, basketball court, boxing and wrestling rooms. Dances were held in the gym. I did not even go to the dances until my second—my senior—year. I loved strutting around in my Sewanee Military Academy uniform, cadet gray and all brass buttons. Girls loved it too. The SMA cadets were allowed, probably encouraged, to invite their girlfriends to "the mountain," as Sewanee was called. They came for the dances, which were held two or three times a year. I did not invite a girl until my last opportunity to do so, in May 1935 when I was a senior. I simply had not met a girl I wanted to invite. My choice was a little blonde Memphian named Mary Ann Williams. I don't remember how we met, but we fell pretty hard for each other. I was sixteen and she was about the same age. She lived in Memphis in a group of apartments, which are still standing, on Cleveland, south of Union. The other fellows had their girls up. We did a lot of dancing. The girls boarded with Sewanee families or innkeepers. Most prominent among the latter was Miss Johnny Tucker. She called her hostelry Tuckaway. The front porches of the homes were wide and long and furnished with benches. A great deal of necking went on, couples oblivious of other couples. Landladies removed themselves, but maintained a discreet distance in order to ensure that nothing tragic happened.

My indulgent mother brought Mary Ann up to Sewanee for commencement. Sometime that year I'd been promoted to the rank of corporal. For weeks I'd been looking forward to their visit, with the opportunity to show off my new stripes. But something happened. One evening I was standing duty as Officer of the Deck, part of my newly assigned responsibilities. Officially I was serving as Corporal Spence, but to my friends and classmates I was still

Happy John. Some of my fellow cadets approached saying they wanted to go to the movies, even though they had not earned that privilege. I told them to go ahead. Later I was caught and summarily demoted back to the lowly rank of private. I was also put to walking punishment tours. I was walking off the last of my punishment when Mother and Mary Ann arrived from Memphis. The Hugginses had come from Murfreesboro. It was a big affair. Luckily, my solo marching was being performed on a small field behind the barracks, out of sight of nearly everyone. My disgrace never came to the attention of my guests, and I suffered no real embarrassment. And yet, looking back now, I see that the event proved a precursor to an eerily similar one four years hence, one far more embarrassing for my kin and damaging to me.

That night we cadets took our dates "out to the cross." Erected on the west brow of Monteagle Mountain, the Christian cross was visible for many miles; it had been put up as a memorial to the "sons of Sewanee" who were killed in World War I. It must have been twenty or thirty feet tall, made out of stone painted white. Everybody in the valley west could see this great white cross. During the hours of the scheduled dance, the cross became the site of— what do we say?—the courting, the lovemaking, the necking of generations of university and academy students and their dates.

Chapter Six

College

When I was sixteen years old, I enrolled at Southwestern College in Memphis. The college (now Rhodes College) had come to Memphis from Clarksville, Tennessee, in 1925. In 1935 when I enrolled, the student body was still very small, around four hundred students.

In those days everybody thought you had to join a fraternity. I got three bids. I joined my father's fraternity, Kappa Sigma, because two dear friends ahead of me in the college were doing the rushing, as it is called. One fraternity that did not bid for me was Sigma Alpha Epsilon. It was richer and fancier, and had more of the sons of prominent Memphis families. The Sigma Alpha Epsilon chapter at Southwestern was, in some minds, the top fraternity. But Kappa Sig had more of the out-of-town boys as members. We had built the first fraternity house on the campus; the SAEs were close behind and built a larger house, but Kappa Sig seemed to fit me better. The fraternity wasn't demanding or time consuming, but I took seriously my fraternity membership, and I had a job preparing that year's pledges for admission to the fraternity.

This was my freshman year. I had enthusiasms. I got interested in things. I didn't participate in intramural sports, but I did take part in drama. I played Judas Iscariot in a play. I think we performed it in a church or two. It was clear to all that I showed promise.

Still, I had no sense of using time. I didn't like to finish things. I went trotting right on along, from being a freshman, sophomore, junior, senior. The incompletes I ignored.

Friends have blamed the professors for failure to provide oversight, or for not demanding more of me. My life was certainly affected by not having a father. Being a boy without a father, you don't know what you're missing. People tell you later on. My mother was the most superb woman who ever lived, but a teenage boy was more than she could handle. She didn't say "John, sit down. Do your work. No more dating until you've caught up. Quit chasing girls." She watched me sadly as I floated along, failing to realize the seriousness of life. I ended up with a very sorry college record.

I seem to have repressed memories of my school failures, though I do retain a vivid memory of extracurricular events. During my sophomore year, January 1937 was cold and very wet, which led to record flooding in Arkansas and Tennessee. Thousands of refugees arrived from across the river and the flood areas outside the city. I was working for the NYA (National Youth Administration), earning thirty cents per hour. I worked at the fairgrounds, where hundreds of people slept on the concrete floor of big open rooms. I also raked leaves and cut grass on the Southwestern campus.

That summer, between my sophomore and junior years, I worked in a bakery, the Taystee Bakery on Monroe. My job was pulling pans from the rotating racks of the ovens. You had to keep track, because the bread could not be allowed to go around a second time. It was the hottest and maybe the most dangerous work I ever did. We sweated so profusely the company supplied us with salt tablets, a practice of that day.

I had an active social life, too. Besides the regular college fraternity, we also had a secret fraternity that was an outright drinking fraternity. It was such a brief thing, this fraternity, which is just as well. I don't know whether the college officials found out and busted it up or not. I knew there were other illicit activities available. Memphis still had its whorehouses in those days too. I don't know when they were shut down; probably around 1940 (at least the more obvious ones). Mulberry Street, which is the small north-south street that runs along the east side of the Chisca Hotel, was made famous or infamous in Faulkner's *Sanctuary* as a place of assignation, or whorehouse. But I never was a customer. I once went inside, timidly and briefly, with an older friend.

I was chasing girls all the time. Chasing them and catching them. They liked me. We didn't have sex. Nobody had sex much in that time. We kissed, but the hands didn't go very far. I will say only they went below the collarbone. But only a little bit. I was a little naive. I admired these women. I genuinely liked them. I thought they were beautiful and precious, and they liked me. But we didn't—you know, it just wasn't the thing. Certainly there were those who did have sex, but not many.

Double dates were popular means of courting in those days. There would be one automobile and you'd be lucky to have a gallon of gas, so you'd maybe go to Fortune's and have an ice cream soda or something, drive around, and go home. We entertained in the homes of our dates.

I had a series of girlfriends named Jane. There was Jane Letterer. There was Mary Jane Ackok. There was Jane Reed, Jane Harsh, and Jane Level. Jane Level was the girlfriend that to this day I can say to myself, "What a fool you were to not hang onto her." She was a great person, really a great person. It was just boyish folly that I didn't know to keep her closer. Jane Level was president of Chi Omega. She was a year ahead of me, senior class. A beautiful girl, handsome girl. We were pretty conspicuous then. I didn't mind. We made a spectacle of ourselves at a dance. I borrowed my godfather's big Buick and his chauffeur. Jane wore her great long white dress and I wore my tails. At the ball everybody was delighted to see Jane and me flaunt our elegance. It was a small society. My mother was not wealthy, but we were always in the upper social set and just took these things for granted. Jane was a wonderfully popular person. After all, you couldn't do much better than be president of Chi Omega. I didn't have many claims to distinction. We led the ball that time.

In the summer of 1938, prior to my senior year, I landed my first real job: I worked at an icehouse and drive-in grocery shop on Summer Avenue. Finding the job took me six weeks of walking the streets. This was in the days before air-conditioning—I tried to sleep in the Kappa Sig basement to escape the heat. It didn't work too well. It was a seven-nights-a-week, twelve-hours-a-night job paying two dollars a night at first. For some reason the managers decided to give us attendants a commission on the ice sales. I think I made as much as ninety dollars a month.

Mother was teaching at New York's Hunter College that summer. Sister Anne was in Murfreesboro. I was alone at 1422 Faxon, except for Minnie Mae, who came in to clean and do some cooking for me. I did Minnie Mae wrong when some money disappeared. I blamed her, and insisted she replace the few dollars that went missing. I might have been right, but I should have overlooked it. We never had a better or more loyal servant than Minnie Mae, whatever her shortcomings were.

Another of my misdeeds later that summer was to take the Hugginses' new "four holer" Buick, the largest Buick then made, I believe, and race it. With four or five of my exciting contemporaries in the car, on a dark night on a two-lane road, I drove that car as fast as it would go. The speedometer registered ninety-six miles per hour. This little adventure never came to the attention of my elders.

I quit the icehouse job in time to begin my senior year. My advisor, Dr. Amacker, asked me to "read for distinction" in political science. This is something you don't get to do unless you show ability. There's one higher level, reading for honors, which I didn't make. The professors saw a person with some brains and potential, and encouraged me to do it. I failed to do that, and I can't explain why. I started out to do it but fell by the wayside, somehow. I can't blame Dr. Amacker for that.

But there I was. I had forty-two hours of incomplete courses. The college folk screwed up in not riding herd on guys like me. Because of my widely recognized academic intelligence, the adults around me thought I was able to keep track of my own progress. The fact is, I was very young to be in college—two years younger than most. Someone should have said, "Hey, John, we're not going to let you go into the senior class until you make up these incompletes. You can't read for distinction. You have all this unfinished work." I was sort of at loose ends. Everyone thought I was bright enough to see this for myself, but I needed guidance.

What was I doing to acquire so many incompletes? Along with reading—I was quite taken with the experience of learning, just not with test taking or homework—I did a fair amount of drinking. I was reckless. I didn't become an alcoholic, but I drank a good deal. I also, as noted, spent a lot of time chasing girls and generally cutting up. And there were other reasons.

Southwestern was a Presbyterian college. Everybody had to take Bible class. There were two Bible courses: freshman and senior. I don't think I ever took the senior course. I was always late to chapel. Walking to school, I often arrived at Palmer Hall after the doors to the auditorium were locked. This earned me demerits, which added up. (Most of my classmates charitably expressed the thought that my failure was from the demerits I received from being late to chapel, but I knew it was more than that. I've thought a lot about it. I just must have been very heedless.)

Lacking supervision, I spent too much time digging deeply into my subjects and not enough time completing assignments on them. Even had I graduated, I had no plans to go to work, to get a job. I was, almost certainly, very immature. I heard no one call me that then, but I do so label myself now. I won no honors that I can recall. I dated too many girls, drank too much whisky, did too few term papers. I was just having too good a time. I call it my courting and drinking period. I was pretty wild. I once brought a whisky bottle into the classroom, put it on the wooden ledge outside an open window, and took a swig every now and then. The professor, needless to say, was not amused. It was an ill-managed time.

So, no, I didn't graduate from Southwestern when I was supposed to. My mother and her sister and brother-in-law were terribly disappointed and probably angry. But what do you do with a foolish twenty-year-old? As for taking another year, there was the matter of money. Who wanted to shell out any more money for a guy who'd already misused his time? It was my mother's money, and my Uncle Jesse's. I also had the little trust from my father that my mother nurtured carefully and invaded very rarely. We drew on it a hundred here, a hundred there, but it was still almost intact in 1939.

It was actually worse than simply not graduating. Jesse and Nannee came down from Murfreesboro to see me graduate. But of course I didn't. I wasn't even out there with my classmates. It was ghastly. Mother didn't come to the graduation; she knew I'd not be there. I must have been a horrible son. I didn't think enough about her. I cringe whenever I recall how Jesse and Nannee drove down from Murfreesboro that day. Jesse intended to give me a car as a graduation present. On the big day, he and Nannee drove the car to Memphis. Great was their chagrin to learn, on arriving, that their nephew John was not going to graduate. They drove that car back to Murfreesboro without any words being said. It must have been a shattering experience for them.

Also on that day I gave my close friend Billy Kelly a gold Hamilton wristwatch (purchased with my earnings from my summer job). I inscribed our names on the back of it: mine, Billy's, and Sam's. I never heard a reaction. Billy accepted it, then he went his way. That was the last time I saw him. He was getting married and going to work. This was in 1939. He and his wife had been sweethearts all through Southwestern, and ended up in Dyersburg, Tennessee. They had a couple of sons who were well educated and very successful. But I never saw him again, and often wondered why. He had a friendship with another classmate of ours, Ed French, an interesting fellow. Ed was on football scholarship. He played pretty good football, did good work academically, and ended up in medical school. Ed was an ultraconservative for reasons I'll never know and don't much care about.

Whether that affected Billy and separated us, I don't know. It might have been his embarrassment about the watch, but I don't think that's what parted us. Maybe we had a different political orientation, one I didn't recognize.

Chapter Seven

Working

I was a twenty-year-old college dropout with absolutely no idea of what to do with myself when my resourceful, forgiving mother thought to farm me out, literally. My cousin, Jim Robertson, was the owner-operator of a fertile farm of five hundred or more acres in a bend of the St. Francis River east of Lake City, Arkansas. He and his wife agreed to try to make a farmer of me. Cousin Jim had a son, also named Jim or James, an only child about my age. I shared a room with him. I recall that he was not too happy to do so. I suppose, thinking of it today, it was an imposition on Cousin Jim's wife as well. But their son probably benefited from the association with a city-bred fellow like me.

I liked farming. Although I didn't make any money (after all, Cousin Jim was giving me three meals and lodging), I did not mind sweating and working. There were several black hands. One was named Roosevelt, and he had been to the North sometime in the past. A lot of blacks had gone north early in the century; then Depression hit, so they'd come back south. They were pleased to find employment. Roosevelt was a good field hand and a pleasant man. In those days, the adult Roosevelts among blacks were obviously named for the Republican Roosevelt, Theodore, not Franklin.

We planted a variety of crops: cotton, corn, sweet potatoes, and watermelons. Jim was trying very hard to be as diversified as economically possible. The practice was a lot more popular then than it is now. It seems that farmers have decided in the last thirty years they don't have to be diversified.

Land restoration was one of the goals of the New Deal, along with encouraging farmers to practice conservation.

Cousin Jim plowed his cotton and other crops with mules and a tractor; mostly with the mules that season. I held the handles of a cultivator (a tool used at the sides of the rows to eliminate the sprouted weeds) behind a pair of mules; the cultivator was a heavy plow, and heavier still to guide.

There is a hazard to walking behind mules as one plows with them. They don't urinate while walking, they have to stand still for that. But they can otherwise relieve themselves. And they can fart. If they've failed to digest some corn, you might just get hit in the forehead with a flying grain of corn. It happened to me.

Jim must have had twenty-five or thirty mules. We were very solicitous, trying to be kind to the mules, because it was easy to overwork them. Especially with certain equipment that pulled harder than other equipment. We'd plow maybe forty-five minutes, stop to rest the mule for fifteen minutes, and go at it again. Mules stand heat better than horses, but they can take only so much of it. It was our practice, when using two mules in harness together, to take a third mule to the field with us. We'd stop every so often, take one mule out to rest him, and put the spare one in. What about the men? They just had to take it, mostly.

While working the fields, I would often daydream of Saturday afternoons in Jonesboro, a town about 12 miles away. And of the beer hall. A cold beer in a cool, shady bar was something to think about. I never drank enough to be intoxicated; it was just such a satisfying drink after a week of sweating in the fields. Young Jim did not join me in the beer parlor.

Cousin Jim had been injured years before and was lame. He did not plow. He probably would not have even if he hadn't been lame. He was the owner, the boss. He supervised from a one-mule, open buggy. His bad leg sort of stuck out the side. He was a good man, a modern farmer.

One of the misfortunes of that summer fell upon a fine crop of watermelons. When Jim took them to the railroad station to ship to market, only then did he discover that the freight charge to Water Valley, Mississippi, where they would be sold, exceeded the proceeds of the sale. Railroads were still doing their thing then.

The Robertsons were highly regarded socially, so young Jim and I could date the belles of Jonesboro. They lived on Jonesboro's main residential street, a wide thoroughfare shaded by trees and lined with comfortably stodgy, two-story, brick houses. One girl I dated, a very pretty girl, was deaf. But we managed to communicate quite well, moving on to some pretty passionate embraces. No sex. Not even considered.

That summer I did a terrible thing. There was an old Model T sitting unused gathering dust in Cousin Jim's barn. I said, "Let me see if I can get it running." It started up, and I took off with it and got as far as Jonesboro. Something went wrong with it. I parked the car in a two-story garage and never went back. I just abandoned that automobile. If Jim missed it, he never said anything about it.

In September 1939, the war in Europe started. The outbreak made a deep impression on me. What would happen? How would it affect me? What should I do about it? I don't mean I agonized, pondered long, or stayed awake over it. I just knew it was the biggest event of my first twenty years. One afternoon on the radio we heard about the German tanks rolling into Poland. I remember standing on the low back steps of our house at 1422 Faxon thinking that I was alone. Not lonely. Just alone.

I did not immediately volunteer for the military. Instead, I looked for a job. I came to know Harry Weiss, a Jewish lumber broker with an office in the Commerce Title Building on Main Street in Memphis. Harry's partner had recently died, and I think Harry did not like looking at his old friend's empty chair. The man had been the salesperson for the American Appraisal Company.

So Harry offered me his friend's place and his vocation. I don't know how I learned about it, or why I was accepted; maybe nobody else wanted the job.

I was supposed to call on the richest families in Memphis and persuade them that, if they had a fire, they would collect a lot more insurance if they'd had their belongings appraised. I took the job on commission, no pay. I worked at it, stayed with it eight or nine months. I spent the winter of 1939–1940 ringing doorbells, going all over Memphis to the wealthy homes and never got anywhere. I never made the first sale. It sounds rough, but it really wasn't too bad.

I was going with Toni Noce at this time, daughter of Major Noce, chief of the Memphis District Corps of Engineers. He was a quiet type as far as my dealing with him went. He was a Catholic, Italian, West Pointer. He had married a New England Yankee Unitarian, a nice woman. Their daughter, Toni, and I had quite a hot romance. I guess she broke it off because she figured there was only trouble ahead. You know, we'd end up having sex or something like that. I wasn't really trying. We were passionate, we were in love, puppy love, maybe. It got too torrid, I think. She blew the whistle on it. I asked her why, but I didn't get an answer.

I was still living at 1422 Faxon. By then we had a telephone. In the big city of Memphis, it was natural to have one. I abused it during my teenage courtship years. I'd sit and call the girls. Initially we had a voice phone, a standup one with an earpiece. Our number was 209, I believe. Later we jumped from 209 to 20629. That remained the number until they went to seven digits. I don't remember when that happened.

In the spring of 1940, I found another job, this with Robert Brinkley Snowden, eccentric foe of Boss Ed Crump, a politician with a powerful—and some said crooked—political machine. Snowden was reared in the stone castle on Central at Lamar that bears his family name. He was also an Arkansas planter and a venture capitalist. (Some say Crump "ran him out of town." I doubt it.) Snowden had got into the frozen locker business. He needed a salesman. I proposed a cattle-raising deal with him that I never carried out, but the idea convinced him I was smart. He sent me to Gibson County, Tennessee, to sell farmers on frozen food lockers; they were to rent them in a storefront locker plant in Milan, Tennessee.

I took a room in Milan. I must have gotten there by bus. I visited the farmers, traveling on foot. I walked the county roads all day, every day, going to the farmhouses. Gibson County was, and perhaps still is, the county that produces more vegetables than any other in these parts. Farmhouses were closer together here than probably anywhere else in the Mid-South. And the farmers were, many of them, of German ancestry. That may have inclined them to small holdings and intensive production. Again, I was a failure as a salesman.

After leaving the sales job, I decided I would become an aircraft engine mechanic. The government was subsidizing that sort of thing. This was in 1940 and 1941. For a few months I attended an aircraft engine mechanic school in Whitehaven. I was the most inept member of the class. I was among guys who had more knowledge about engines in their left hands than I'd ever learned. I saw that I was not exactly among my social equals; not that I was superior to them, just different. I liked them, and I think they liked me. But I had not grown up making engines work, and I did not then (nor do I now) have the analytical mind that a good mechanic has. I never earned the A&E license that was needed for a job with an airline or for becoming an Air Force specialist.

My sister Anne was a very intelligent person and did not get into the trouble I did. She made excellent grades in school and college. She had graduated from Memphis's Central High School in 1934, then had two years at Sweetbriar College in Virginia. The Hugginses paid for her tuition for two years, and then Anne came to Southwestern as a junior and joined the Kappa Delta sorority, which was not as highly regarded as the others. Of course, I was at Southwestern at this time too. I did not work as hard as I should have to get her dates, and she didn't have many. In 1938 she graduated from Southwestern with honors. She worked downtown as a secretary.

Sometime around then, I heard about a civilian pilot training program[14] down at the municipal airport. It was an early effort to begin to train military pilots. That is, you could join the army with the prospect of becoming a pilot and an officer and a gentleman. The draft had been put into place in 1940, and my high number put me at risk, so I signed up. We flew small single engine Pipers and Aeronca airplanes. My instructor, young and inexperienced, was always shouting at me. He instilled fear where there should have been none.

Many believed we would be going to war, but no one knew precisely when. Pearl Harbor was six months away when I completed cadet training. In late May, I was on a train for Little Rock. Joe Jones, Hays Brantley, and Bill Harbison, all from Memphis, went, too. There we were sworn in on May 31, 1941, as Aviation Cadets in the U.S. Army. I've never known why Memphians were sent to Little Rock to be sworn in.

As new enlistees, we boarded a train bound for Corsicana, Texas, a small town with hospitable folk. At the municipal airport we began our basic flight training for primary training with civilian instructors. We flew the PT-19, a low-wing monoplane. Some trained in biplanes. I did not do well, but I managed to solo barely under the eight hours maximum allowed training time.

Our instructors were civilians operating under a government contract. There was nothing military about it, except that we were enlisted men in the army. Our flight training went on through June, July, and August of 1941. I had the hope and expectation that I would become a pilot. We all wanted to be pilots, of course.

I was sent on with most of the others to Randolph Field at San Antonio, known as "the West Point of the Air." There we flew low-wing monoplanes with a 450 hp radial engine. They were called BT-9Ds. I just didn't have the guts for such a large airplane—I washed out. I got shipped on to Maxwell Field in Alabama with all the other washouts. There they put us in storage, pending decisions on what to do with us. Things weren't going the way I'd envisioned. But it was too late to turn back.

If I'd not gone into the military, Lord only knows what my life would have been like. Going into the army air force was my privilege, because I had acquired some college education. The Army Air Forces Aviation Cadet Training Program was just a godsend for me. Things went straight up from there.

This is a terrible thing to say, I suppose, but either way—pilot or navigator—the war was one of the best things that ever happened to me. Here was a college washout who ended up going into combat in the European theater of war and achieving the rank of captain as a flying officer. Becoming a hero to some. Later I would be given as rich and sundry opportunities as anyone, far greater than most young men my age.

In light of what later occurred, I see my adolescent failures as a training ground for the war and for my civic life that followed. No matter what happened, my mother and those dearest to me would continue to value me. Their kindness taught me that despite failure, I could undertake any challenge. Rejection was someone else's burden.

Part II

Crucible

Chapter Eight

First In, First Out

Luck, I now realize, played an enormous role in my war experience, nowhere so obvious as in the timing of my birth. Born in 1919, I joined the army before America's mobilization into World War II. With the flood of volunteers and draftees who followed behind, I stood at the head of nearly every line I joined. I was awarded my wings and began my combat missions before many Americans had had time to get overseas. I and my fellow bomb group members were the first in, first over, first back, and first out. Rewards often come to those who stay one step ahead. That too is a matter of luck. During my first few months in the Army Air Corps, though, luck was not on my side.

The check ride happened in late summer. It was called the "washout flight." My examiner was an Army captain I'd never laid eyes on. I once heard another instructor say about a student pilot, "He might make it or he won't make it." He could easily have been talking about me. I don't recall the details of the flight, other than I didn't make a very good landing, and maybe didn't respond properly. Right after the check ride I was told to expect orders transferring me to Maxwell Field. Nothing was mentioned about the reason for the transfer. It was crushing. I think I just didn't do a good job. I may have gone into it with a defeatist attitude. Today I blame the loudmouthed instructor I'd had in Memphis. He made me fear flying. I believe he thought I was a snob, which I don't think I was. He was brutal. "Do this! Do that, damn it!" Scared me to death. I wrote my mother about it, but I don't think I told anyone else. This was a major defeat for me, but certainly not my first nor my last. And, as fate would have it, this event opened a door in my life.

Four or five hundred cadets were kept idle for a time, no one in authority having planned our next use. As washouts, we were dispirited fellows all. Because of my earlier military training as a cadet at Sewanee, I was given command of several hundred of my fellow cadets. I had a voice that easily carried a half-mile or so, and I got my troops here and there in good order. But the military's love of rank and seniority got me in trouble. I responded roughly to an officious upper classman and ended up losing my command. It was no great loss.

Along with my demotion, I was placed on base restriction. But I happened to know a local family, the Joneses, whose son was a fellow alumnus of Southwestern University in Memphis. The Joneses were doing their patriotic duty being nice to military guys. They also had an attractive daughter who graced their home. They offered lunches with excellent food. On a weekend in December, I was invited to be their guest at Sunday lunch. I decided there wasn't much risk in leaving the base as there was no system in place to account for who was around. So I walked through the gates into town without checking out.

Sunday meal was set out in the dining room of their modest house. Six of us sat around the table: the parents, the girl and her brothers, and myself. It was about noon, and we were having our meal and listening to the radio. An announcer interrupted the program to say the naval fleet at Pearl Harbor was under Japanese attack. I figured I'd better return to the base. I didn't bother to tell them I was AWOL. It was natural to say, "Well, I better get back." Nothing came of my unauthorized absence.

Everyone around my age knows where he was on December 7, 1941. I was AWOL, enjoying a Sunday lunch in town.

Soon afterward, I was hospitalized. I'd had some dental work done, which led to an infected wisdom tooth. After admission to the hospital, things only got worse. I was in a semiconscious state for a few days. Somewhere in my delirium I received a Dear John letter from my Memphis girlfriend, which did not help my recovery. The pain was lightened considerably when one of the student nurses, a handsome brunette from Iowa, fell for me. She was an officer, and I was not an officer. Officers and cadets were not supposed to fraternize, but we fraternized anyhow. It didn't get very serious.

After I recovered, I was free to go into town. One of my pleasures in Montgomery was an occasional visit to an elite café that served New York sirloin steaks. I was living high on the hog. The townspeople arranged weekend dances at a downtown hotel, and encouraged their daughters to come. They were sponsored by the USO and were well chaperoned. There I met a tall, slender blond. Her name was Mary Binyon Wheeler, and her nickname was Weetsie. She was a student of modern dance at Judson College in Marion, Alabama, and moved as lightly as air. She hailed from Eutaw, Alabama, a small county seat in Greene County, described in later years as "the poorest county in the state." Eutaw was a slow, sleepy town. Weetsie's father ran a small restaurant there on the courthouse square, City Café on the Square. They lived a block and a half away. Though poor, socially they were one of the leading families. There were relatives who lived in a classic antebellum plantation home.

Almost all our subsequent courtship was by mail, as I had finally received an assignment: navigation school in California, likely on account of the high scores I had gotten on written tests. When my orders to California came, I asked Weetsie if she would meet me at the Tutwiler Hotel, Birmingham's best. We could be together until midnight. "I'll be there," she said.

We met in the lobby, nervous, embarrassed. We registered for a room. Once there, we were happily at ease. We were aware of the passing of time, of the time for the bus, the time to part. I had a shower, donned my uniform, as Weetsie, too, readied herself to meet the world outside. Our last, inerasable memories of each other came at the bus terminal, she sitting alone, waving to me as I stood on the asphalt. She sat by a window, her face almost on the glass, smiling, gesturing.

I headed out to Mather Field, on the outskirts of Sacramento, California. Traveling with me were two young cavalry officers wearing their shiny tall boots. They were straight out of the army's advanced training at Fort Leavenworth.

On New Year's Eve, riding the train to Sacramento, I met a good-looking young woman, hardly more than a girl. She had whiskey. We drank. We kissed, caressed. She headed for the restroom; whether men's or women's I don't know, taking me with her. Sixty years later, I don't remember as much as I wish I did about that girl; we corresponded for some months, very busy months in intensive training and miles apart. Then we lost touch. Wartime makes us act, as we would not in peacetime. We knew we would be sent hundreds of miles away from these momentary friendships that might never be rekindled. Perhaps we were thinking that we might soon be dead in combat.

My goal at Mather Field was to earn my Army commission, along with the status of a flying officer. We flew training missions and the instructors were superb. They were civilians; I don't believe they were ex-military. They were sharp teachers, good teachers. We trained in the air, working with compasses. We learned how to use the drift meter, which measured sideways drift and, by inference, the wind. We learned celestial navigation. We learned the fine art of dead reckoning. Everyone who completed training was well qualified to guide our bombers to their targets.

We knew we'd be going to war, we just didn't know which war. We'd just declared war on Japan, and the Germans had declared war on us. But at this point, there wasn't any talk about actually joining the European theater and helping the British.

During that time, another illness eerily intervened and almost cost me my goal. In March, I experienced another toothache, this in my front teeth. They'd been pushed in ten years earlier during a neighborhood football game on the well-house lot, and now they were starting to fall out. The base dentist took one look at them and said he could repair my teeth but it might take six months. That's how long I'd be delayed in getting my commission. I decided that this was just typical military bureaucracy. I went into town and looked up a private practitioner. His name was Orlando J. Casellis. He yanked out four rotten teeth, producing very little pain or after-effects. Army regulations said you couldn't have too many missing teeth, so they had to be replaced. Dr. Casellis installed a bridge. He completed the whole job in less than a week.

At last, I had orders to report to the 38th Reconnaissance Group at Gowen Field in Boise, Idaho. I traveled by train to Ogden, Utah, and then by bus to Boise, taking in the beauty of the Western mountains and plains. I recall desert antelopes running alongside the bus.

When on April 1, 1942, I received my commission as Second Lieutenant, U.S. Army, along with my aerial observer's wings, I ducked into a pay phone at the hotel in Boise and called Judson College and asked for Weetsie. Buoyed by my promotion, I proposed to her. She said yes.

The weeks at Gowen Field were pleasant. High over the deserts of Oregon and Washington we practiced the art of aerial navigation. Here it was all military, no civilian instructors. We flew some kind of twin-engine airplane, large enough to serve as a flying classroom. I recall one maneuver called "compensating the compass" where we flew in different headings, maybe sixteen in all. Magnetic compasses weren't all that accurate, but they were quite dependable if you understood their quirks. You had to know the correction factor for each heading. Such compasses would become indispensable for navigating over the long distances to and from our European targets.

The spring days passed while I went about my duties as a navigator. We had these scares about the Japanese attacking the West Coast, and so they'd send us off to San Diego or wherever to fly patrol on the Pacific Ocean. We'd fly a thousand miles at sea, looking for Japanese submarines.

In late June, I had an opportunity to practice my skills aboard a B-17 bomber embarked on a cross-country flight. With the help of my squadron mates, it was arranged to fly me to the Air Force base at Smyrna, Tennessee. There was a small airfield located half way between Nashville and Murfreesboro. I'd have a few days leave there, so I sent word to Weetsie to meet me there.

We were married on June 29, 1942, in Murfreesboro in St. Paul's Episcopal church on East Main, the church in which I had been christened twenty-three years before. Everyone, full of charity, romance, and patriotism, made all efforts to stage a formal wedding. Weetsie and her mother would have to travel, however they could, the nearly three hundred miles from Eutaw. My sister Anne would be Weetsie's maid of honor; her husband-to-be, Lawrence F. Eyerly, would be best man. Cousin Cornelia and her husband Dr. Matt Murfree would house the Wheelers in their spacious home just a block and a half from the church; my aunt and uncle, Nannee and Jesse, could host the Spences. In the event, Weetsie's mother came in by bus, but Mr. Wheeler couldn't make it; couldn't leave his restaurant, I suppose. My Uncle Jesse would give the bride away instead.

One small shadow was that Sis's wedding was to take place in the same small church the next day. She was, understandably, disgruntled that I should have popped in, fairly unscheduled, the night before. She felt we were "taking the shine off" her event. I don't know that our wedding lessened the quality of her wedding to Lawrence; I hope not.

On the evening of June 29th, Murfreesboroans, family and friends, filled the little church. Weetsie was emotionally and physically spent by the time the day arrived. She was slightly ill, but recovered in time for our wedding. She arrived at the church door a vibrant, radiant, and smiling bride, a gauze veil on her blonde hair, wearing a snowy wedding gown and train. After the wedding, in a borrowed car, we drove an hour or so to the hotel at Monteagle, on the edge of the Cumberland Plateau a few miles east of Sewanee, where I had been a cadet in high school.

We returned to Murfreesboro the next day, eager to begin our lives together. We joined the wedding party of Anne and Lawrence; then boarded the westbound train to Alamogordo, New Mexico, where I would be stationed. We continued the honeymoon on the train. It was a long ride. We shared a Pullman berth, and when we arrived in Alamogordo, we rented a room in a boarding house. We ate our meals at a little café. I don't know how long we were there. Things were moving fast in those days.

Soon the 303rd moved to another desert airfield, this one at Biggs Field, outside El Paso, Texas. Weetsie found a nice apartment on the second floor at 1414 North Predras Street. I remember my wife and I setting up housekeeping. It was a quiet and pleasant few weeks.

In El Paso, we received our flight crew assignments. We began to get to know each other. Our pilot was Sandy Sanderson, a very amiable, low-key sort of a guy. He was a big man, taller than I. So was our copilot Dale Bowman. Big men were often chosen to pilot four-engine bombers, the B-17s and B-24s. Sandy and Dale were both cheerful and pleasant people. Both wore "shaved tail" insignia and were ranked as second lieutenants, as were Grady Ward, the bombardier, and I. Dale was from California, a graduate of Stanford. Sandy, from Illinois, had a less elegant education, but he was from a good family.

We didn't yet have our own airplanes. All the crews took turns flying the same B-17. These were in short supply, and thus they flew twenty-four hours a day. Long days and often long nights, I was in the air on training flights. The summer air was torrid, and the B-17s were scorching to the touch. Once airborne and soaring thousands of feet above the ground, though, they became iceboxes. Crewmembers hurriedly donned fleece-lined jackets, the garments that postwar became treasured souvenirs worn by wives, sons, and daughters.

By the fall of 1942, the crew had become seasoned; it was time to pick up our own plane. Ground crews had already shipped out for England, while we air crews departed by troop train for Battle Creek, Michigan. The wives were left to make their own way to wherever they chose. In most cases it was home. Weetsie made her way alone back to Eutaw.

At Kellogg Field in Battle Creek, the 303rd flight crews finally received our own planes. Our airplane, a B-17F, bore the serial number 41-24603. It was a beautiful bird, and all it needed now was a name. Most bombers were named by the pilot, but Sandy insisted our name be chosen in a democratic manner. We consulted all around and voted to name ours the Green Hornet. At the time, I didn't know about the Green Hornet radio program. The "green" related to the color of the airplanes. The United States was still camouflaging bombers against the possibility of the Germans bombing our airfields. (Later on the German air force was depleted to the point they were no longer capable of reaching our bases. Also, in the air you were tracked by your contrails, not by the sight of the plane itself. Eventually, planners did away with the paint, leaving the planes bare aluminum. This all occurred after my time.)

One day we were told to fly from Battle Creek to Dayton, Ohio, to pick up our personal gear. The supply people treated us royally, giving us whatever equipment we asked for. "What do you guys want?" they asked. I picked out a wonderful navigation watch, a Hack Swiss watch I wore for forty years. In addition to its beauty, it kept the same time as everybody else's.

As we neared our departure date from the States, someone suggested a one-day farewell flight. Sandy and Dale agreed. We would fly our plane over as many of the crewmembers' homes as possible, on whatever fuel our tanks would hold. This all had to happen in one day. Our hometowns were scattered from Massachusetts to Pennsylvania to Kentucky to Tennessee to Illinois, New Mexico, and California. We didn't get to the homes of those who lived in the west. But we covered a lot of ground. At one point we flew under the Ohio River Bridge at Cairo, Illinois, Sandy's hometown. I was seated in the nose when we flew under the bridge. I had complete confidence in the pilot and copilot. I felt they were first-class pilots and wouldn't really do anything extreme or hazardous. They were responsible guys. I'm sure at any other time we would have been called to account for our stunt, but we never were.

After our return, there were more good-byes to be said. We summoned wives and sweethearts to see us off. Weetsie came by bus from Eutaw to some Indiana town, as near as Greyhound could get her to Battle Creek. We drove up to Battle Creek where we spent a few blissful days and nights together. With our airplane named and outfitted, our wives and sweethearts kissed us good-bye. We were headed off for the war. We hoped that the parting would be temporary—until I completed my twenty-five combat missions or was injured—but we understood it might be final, that I might die. Safe return, injury, or death: I never imagined any other possibilities.

We flew first to Bangor, Maine, where we stayed for a few days. There a photograph was made of our crew standing beneath the wing of the airplane. We continued on to Newfoundland, flying nose to tail in heavy fog up the coast. We waited there for good weather.

On an October night in 1942, beginning at midnight, our group departed for Europe. Thirty-five airplanes would be carrying 350 men along with all the weight in fuel and equipment that a B-17 was able to carry. We took off at one-minute intervals. Over a moonlit landscape, we remained out of sight of each other, each plane performing its own navigation. As navigator of the Green Hornet, I did my best to get us there—Dale and Sandy might have assisted by tuning in to some radio guidance—and was as happy as anyone to see the Irish countryside appearing more or less on time. After six or seven hours of flying, we reached the Irish shore at dawn.

Ireland was a welcome sight. The countryside was so green, with little patches of fields looking like a checkerboard in the morning light. We flew low over the hills, then crossed the Irish Sea and landed in Scotland. There we gassed up and got breakfast. Again we took off singly at intervals to fly to our future base: RAC (Royal Air Corps) Molesworth. We arrived on October 21, 1942. We were met by our ground crew, who had arrived ahead of us. They'd just completed the ocean crossing aboard the HMS Queen Mary, a fast ship placed into service partly for its ability to outrun lurking Nazi submarines.

I'll never forget those days at Molesworth, especially my first introduction to the English capital. In October, soon after our bomb group landed from the States, I hitched a ride into town. My driver dropped me off smack in the middle of the bustling Piccadilly Circus. I was the first in my group to arrive.

It was five o'clock in the afternoon. I went into a coffeehouse filled with women seated at tables. They were beautiful. Two I met easily. One was named Inga Schuler, a German Jewish refugee who lived in an apartment above a café; I would spend some time with her. She invited me to her parents' home in Hyde Park Square, an elegant series of apartment houses not far from downtown. I think she used more than one name; I was more Inga's conquest than she was mine. I was married; many of us were, but we were thousands of miles and many combat missions away from our wives. Nearly all the married guys found themselves a girlfriend in England, most of us within forty-eight hours after our arrival. It was the single guys who floundered around looking.

Because I was in the vanguard, I was appointed to find quarters for all of us. I was thinking of the economy, but nevertheless considered the rooms I'd booked more than adequate, even elegant. The other guys said, "Aw, heck, we want finer stuff than this." So they moved to the Dorchester and other fancy hotels.

At Molesworth and in London, we were all together as before, except now we were stationed near the front. Only half-heartedly did we consider ourselves to be ready for combat and all its eventualities. In fact, we had no idea of what awaited us.

Chapter Nine

What Went Wrong

Our B-17 bomber would be shot down on January 23, 1943, following a run on Nazi submarine pens on France's northern coast.

It was the eighth mission for our plane. Our squadron flew in tight formation with two or three other planes. Counting the other squadrons and bombardment groups, about eighty planes left England that morning. Across the English Channel awaited squadrons of German fighters. We knew—or we hoped—they were as afraid of us as we were of them.

There was a good reason why German fighters might be wary of a fully operational "Flying Fortress," the B-17's official sobriquet. The Fortress had tremendous firepower: each one of the ten crewmembers, save for the pilot and copilot, had one or sometimes two machine guns. The six crewmembers stationed behind the nose were particularly expert with their guns. Miles Jones, tech sergeant, was our radio operator and he also fired a single hand-operated gun through the opening in the radio compartment. Waist gunner Sergeant Swanson—we called him Swanny—and Sergeant Silva each fired a single hand-operated .50-caliber gun. Sergeants Sid Devers and Frank Greene fired power-operated dual machine guns. Greene was ball-turret gunner. (Ball-turret gunners were usually small men because the turret was a tight fit.) Joe Markiewicz, a big, handsome, blonde Polish fellow from Massachusetts, was the tail gunner. He had twin .50s, but they were not power operated. Two more guns were mounted in the nose where Grady Ward and I sat. These single-barrel guns weren't a whole lot of use, but they offered some comfort when the German fighters started coming in.

During a firefight we spoke on the intercom. That way everybody knew where the enemy planes were. I sat in the nose behind the bombardier, with a clear view of what was coming. Over the intercom I might say, "FW coming at two o'clock." Or "FW coming in on the nose." The FW 190 Focke-Wulf fighters, super-powered and very fast, dominated the skies.

At that early stage of the air war, Germany had us outmanned in fighter planes. Those FW 190s gave us a pretty good time. There were also the German Messerschmitts, or ME 109s, sometimes called "bully birds." They were formidable, but not as numerous as the FWs. They were opposed by our own fighter escorts. The escorts were British and consisted of the Hawker Hurricanes and the Spitfires. The Spitfire caught the public's imagination more than the Hurricane did. The Hurricane did more fighting, on account of its longer range. But it was the Spitfire that won the hearts of the Allies, beginning with the Battle of Britain. A Spitfire could get into combat almost as soon as it got off the ground. They were good at defending us from the German fighters, but only to a point due to their limited range. By the time we reached our targets, the escorts had to fall back and return to base, leaving us strictly on our own.

Enemy planes that came directly at us usually were at our altitude. They knew the location of the blind spot where Greene's ball turret was unable to fire. Planes that came in from the side often dived down, so our top gunner might holler something like "two o'clock high." If a fighter was diving in on me, I might yell out "twelve o'clock high." (That phrase was immortalized by a movie that came out after the war. I saw it in 1949 or '50, in Memphis at one of the downtown theaters.) It didn't matter who called out the sighting. Of course, we would recognize each other's voices. We'd been doing this together for some time.

We knew from the very first mission that there was tremendous antiaircraft firepower down there. Their antiaircraft was superb. We really dreaded that. You couldn't see it coming. Most antiaircraft fire was delivered by the German 88 mm cannons, notorious for their accuracy on high-altitude bombers such as ours. Whenever we saw little puffs of black smoke in the sky around us, we knew the gunners had missed. But we couldn't know whether they were aiming at our airplane or at someone else's. We had an inelegant expression for the feeling we experienced while watching the black bursts or, worse, seeing other planes in our formation being hit. We said that our ass was "chewing button holes."

We remained oblivious to the reality of actual combat, mostly on account of our superior attitude. We were the big shots who were going to bomb the Germans by day. The British had bombed by night for years. Americans thought that was sissy stuff. We were going to fly formation and we were going to do precision bombing, which required daylight bombing. This turned out to be a joke. We did not do precision bombing. The lead bombardier, in the lead plane, would do his dead level best to zero in on the target. As for the rest of us, when it came time for the lead plane to drop its bombs, we dropped ours. It was an all-together type of thing.

In truth, daylight bombing was to the enemy's advantage, as it enabled their precision antiaircraft cannons to see and fire onto our airplanes. The Germans couldn't believe their good luck when they saw that we were conducting raids in broad daylight. Their aim with ground fire and tactics with the fighters continued to improve.

The way I felt about going into combat was—I was scared. So was everyone else. I also felt some exhilaration. I was thinking, we're out here. We have the whole United States backing us up and taking care of us. For every one of us in combat, there were twenty military men who never saw a shot fired. There was a pride in knowing that. We felt we had wonderful equipment. We believed the B-17 to be a great plane. We thought it was superior to the B-24, though that plane had more range, was produced in greater numbers, and flew more missions. Ours was the Flying Fortress, which reached the theater first and caught the public's imagination. It was a sturdy, dependable airplane. It could get you home on one engine and half a wing shot off.

Returning to base after a combat mission was a scramble. Once you were out of range of the German fighters, it was every crew for itself. That's when I did my real navigation. No formation, no planes to follow. The British maps were superb. They were plotted at a scale of 1 to 250,000. We would fly low. We would make a gas-saving descent from high altitude, letting the planes drop in. Flying low over England, if you had to put down early, you had airfields all around. Many a plane of ours landed on someone else's airfield.

Once we'd arrived back at the home field, we put down on whatever runway looked open. Runways were going this way and that. We tried to give priority to those planes that were shot up the worst, as well as we could tell. There was some communication between the tower and the planes.

On our first combat mission, we got airborne and out over the channel when something went wrong with an engine. So we turned around and came home. Our wing often had aborts for engine trouble or other malfunctions, such as guns jamming. Or someone might get sick onboard. But the first mission was our only abort.

We flew in a tight formation, and we varied our altitude. But our formations weren't so well thought out. We probably did shoot down our own planes, at times. (Later the formation pattern was changed by General Curtis Lemay. He thought up new ways of having every gun as clear as possible of our own planes.) Also, we didn't have a sufficient number of planes. Some of our planes had been sent down to North Africa. That left us in Europe with only four groups, or about 140 planes. Later on, after I'd left, they put up one thousand planes. They flew fantastic distances, probing deep into Germany, to

Williamsburg, ten-, eleven-, twelve-hour missions. We never got over Germany during my time.

Our targets were railroad yards and submarine pens in France. The submarine pens lay along the coast. The Germans had covered them with thick protective concrete. We could drop bombs on them and make direct hits and still not do much damage. Our best hope was to catch a submarine entering or leaving the pens.

During one of the later missions, we were set upon by a heavy concentration of Nazi fighters. They positioned themselves just out of our machine gun range, moving parallel with our formation. I don't know how they decided when to make their move. I remember cussing at them. "Come on, you son of a bitch, come on over here and let me have a shot at you." This was with my little single-barrel gun. When they saw about as much as they could of our defenses, I suppose, they figured it was time to attack. All of a sudden they started coming in at us. I aimed as best I could and fired, but I don't believe I hit anything. People made a lot of claims about targets hit and planes shot down. I don't remember what our ratio was, but I believe we hit a lot of them. If you saw a plane dropping down and trailing smoke, you figured you hit him. For me, it felt impersonal. I didn't think that I would be killing another guy such as myself. I probably should have, but I didn't. During those intense moments we didn't give a lot of thought to the danger or the consequences. As for the rest of the time, I was scared. I went out scared most of the time.

We got down to London after every couple of combat missions: in the course of October through January, we made about four or five trips. London was very receptive. We would ride down as a group, but still observing the officer-enlisted separation. Officers would go one way, the enlisted men another. I followed my friends' example from our first visit to London, and put up at the fancier hotels. Because we were at war, we always wore our uniforms. The

American uniform was a fresh sight to the English. As I've often said, we were the first in, first over, first back, and first out. Being first, we were received with open arms everywhere. Americans who arrived later wore out the welcome. They became old hat for the Brits, and didn't get quite the same warm reception that we did.

The English women were especially fond of Americans. There were blackouts everywhere at night; and one saw a lot of standup screwing—a couple here, another there.

I had a bicycle at the base. I enjoyed riding around the countryside. I met a really lovely woman, a Mrs. Seeley, one day while I was biking around, a few minutes from the base. I believe it was through a roadman. The practice in England was to have someone—usually an older guy but one physically fit—patrol the miles of road on foot or bicycle. He picked up trash and reported needs for repairs. He was called the roadman. It was the roadman I would sometimes stop and talk to who connected me with the Seeley family. They had rented a former manse at Clapton, very near Molesworth. It was a spacious house with generous grounds. She moved there most likely to escape the London air raids. Her husband was a prisoner of war, an officer captured in North Africa. She lived with her three children and a couple of servants. I was a guest there several times. I just loved being with the children. They were so beautiful and sweet. They had classic names. The girls were Victoria and Alexandria. They had a boy, but I don't remember his name.

She was so interesting, very much upper class. She expected me to have a personal acquaintance with some prominent Americans. She would ask if I knew so-and-so, and I said no I didn't. The place where they were living was so pleasant. Being there was like being in a world without war.

Later, after I was shot down, she came to the base saying, "where is Lieutenant Spence"? They had to tell her I was missing in action. I didn't have sense enough when I got back to go to her and say, "Hey, I made it." I did a lot of stupid, careless things then. I blame it on my youth.

At around 10:00 a.m. on the fateful morning of our eighth mission, pilot Sandy and copilot Dale tested the four engines. Brakes off, we rolled slowly into line with fourteen other planes. We took off, one by one, and fell into formation as we began to climb. The day was sunny. Our time to target was about four hours. Above ten thousand feet, we donned our oxygen masks and electrically heated flight suits. The five rear gunners occupied chilly quarters, especially at high altitudes. Those suits were fashioned out of wool, colored baby blue; they were quite warm.

Soon we were at twenty-five thousand feet, heading toward the target and already taking flak. We steered a straight line amid the deadly black puffs. At 1:45, we dropped our bombs but did not observe any hits. This was not unusual. The heralded Norden bombsight was not all it was cracked up to be. Since the end of the war I've wondered how many civilians our errant bombs may have killed. Then we were too high to be aware of the damage; what we were most concerned about was the flak that the Germans sprayed up around us.

As soon as Grady yelled "bombs away," with flak drawing ever closer, we lost an engine. Then we lost another. With the propellers on the crippled engines feathered to reduce drag, we descended through twenty-two thousand feet. By this time we'd fallen out of formation. German fighters gave us their undivided attention. Nazi pilots had learned very quickly that B-17s flying out of formation were the most vulnerable. A dozen or so FW 190s came in. I shot at one until my gun went out. Sandy and Dale were doing a masterful job of trying to avoid the Nazi fighters. Sandy started taking evasive action, diving toward cloud cover and making violent maneuvers to avoid the fighters, throwing our big old bomber around the sky as if it were a fighter plane. Things were getting tossed around in the airplane.

When it became obvious we weren't going to make it home, Sandy sounded the bailout bell. I joined the bombardier and engineer and headed toward the nearest opening, the forward hatch. Inexplicably, the pilot and copilot remained at the controls. Red hydraulic fluid was spilling everywhere. The number four engine stopped. Another bullet struck the nose.

There were no doors, only the emergency hatch. The radio operator, the next man back, exited the open bomb bay doors. The ball turret gunner simply rolled the ball around and fell out of the turret. The waist gunners either came forward and went through the bomb bay, or maybe went out a window. The tail gunner, Markiewicz, I don't recall how he got out.

Sandy and Dale kept working with the engines. I think they had two of them running when it was finally my turn to jump. I would be the last to leave. I kicked open the hatch. Sandy and Dale hung on. I was chicken. At about 5,500 feet Grady Ward, my companion in the nose, did as ordered. I ripped off my oxygen mask to get free, but still I hung back. I was afraid. I didn't trust my life to that parachute. I worried too, I might hit the guns of the ball turret, left in the down position when Greene bailed out. Sandy and Dale continued wrestling the controls. I hollered something to them, wondering if there was hope. I sat a moment or so with my legs dangling out, trying to get the courage to go. At 4,500 feet I pushed myself out, pulled my ripcord and felt the chute open. I was alone in the heavens.

Chapter Ten

On the Run

With our chutes and life vests gotten rid of, Sid and I had to put distance between ourselves and our landing spot. Nazi planes were flying overhead and we could still hear cars racing about the area. In minutes we were on a narrow dirt road, and soon we reached a paved one that turned out to be the main street of a village; we would learn it was Bourg de Paule. We walked boldly, waving and smiling at quite a few folks standing in their doorways. They seemed to anticipate passersby, but could hardly be expecting American airmen, unless they had seen the descending parachutes. I suppose it was the custom in France to turn out at the sound or sight of a formation of Allied planes in the sky. The Royal Air Force had been continuing their bombing flights in the area, although theirs were almost always flown at night.

Sid and I were wearing our outlandish baby blue flight suits, and smiled hugely if not sheepishly as we waved. We expected the villagers to smile back at us, which they did, even if they did nothing else. We were totally vulnerable because we were in Army Air Force gear. Nearby was a school that had just let out. There were several dozen students, and we waved at them too. We heard a voice behind us. A young girl was waving, yelling, "Reviens!"—"Come back!"—along with other words we didn't know, although it sounded friendly. An older couple stood in a doorway with the girl, and in a moment we were inside the roadside cottage with the three of them.

I spoke French very poorly, but my two years of college French were not far in the past, and I could understand a good deal. We assumed the couple were our hosts, but it was the teenage girl who seemed in charge. A lengthy discussion ensued between the girl and the older couple. They were arguing with her, but their words didn't change anything. "Put on these clothes," she said, handing us some felt pants, blue denim overalls, and jackets. We moved quickly. "And you must not stay on the road." She opened the back door. "Go to the canal," she said, pointing down a long, open slope. We thanked her and the couple alike, and did as we were told. This took us through the fields in a southeast direction, according to our compass. We would be plainly visible for the next two hours before we reached the tree-sheltered banks of the Nantes-Brest Canal.

I didn't know it then, but our first and most essential helper was a seventeen-year-old orphan girl. She had lost her mother at an early age and had been sent away to a convent school. Her father had died the day before and she'd been called home to bury him. This was now her home. That day was her father's funeral and she was giving us his clothes. The older couple were neighbors who had come to console her in her grief. They were a generation older than Jeannette, but she was the boss now.

It was mid-afternoon, a bright, sunny day. Nazi pilots surely could see us if they looked. But Jeannette Gueguec Pennes had made us Bretons with her father's clothes.

We walked in the afternoon sunlight, confident in our sweat-stained famer's clothing. We strode eastward along the bank of the canal. The towpath was the easiest route to follow, being level, wide, and gravel surfaced. We had to wonder if we might meet Nazi guards, but we met no one.

At the time, officers and enlisted men did not mix. A person's rank, and the separation it induced, naturally got in the way of friendships. So my friendship with Sid dates from the day we were shot down. I don't actually know if the friendship was real. He called me "Lieutenant" all the way. I can't recall if I called him Sid, rather than Sergeant. I believe that I did.

He was my age, within a year or so; probably younger. In 1942, when we first met, I was twenty-three. His job description was "engineer," and he had manned the top turret, probably the most powerful gun in the plane. I don't believe Sid had any education beyond high school. He was kin to Lt. Gen. Jacob Devers, who later in the war commanded the 7th Army under General Eisenhower.

Dusk came early that winter afternoon. We took to a paved road and passed through the town of Glomel. On the far side, we spotted a dim firelight from a farmhouse window. We knocked on the door and were admitted. I suppose the whole countryside was alert to the air war over their heads from time to time. That day's spectacular show of falling planes and parachuting airmen made our arrival no surprise to anyone. The family gave us bread and drink, and some eggs to take with us. They told us there were no Germans nearby, and they gave us a map. It was obvious that these folk rightly feared a visit from the Nazis. I told them Sid and I would be leaving.

On the way out into the night, I thought to give the man of the house my flying boots. I wore ordinary street shoes underneath, which I knew would serve me better. The man happily accepted my gift, and gave me the name of a lady in Bonen who he thought might shelter us. Her husband, he said, was a prisoner of war.

We hurried on in the dark. It was chilly, but not numbing; the winter of 1943 was a mild one. We could not have found easier walking in all of France. Nothing is flatter than a canal path. The night was still. The only sound we heard was the crunching of our feet in the gravel.

We naturally feared coming upon a Nazi pillbox placed near the canal. It would be armed with a deadly machine gun. As an officer, I carried a .45 caliber automatic pistol. Sid had no weapon. Would I shoot a Nazi soldier threatening to capture us? A few days later I gave the pistol to a Breton helper, having realized I could not fire a pistol point blank into a human face.

Around midnight we arrived in the town, exhausted. There was no sign of the recommended place. On the town's outskirts we came upon a farmhouse. No one answered our knock. It became a Goldilocks adventure. We discovered a low ceilinged lean-to on the side of the farmhouse. Probing around in the dark we found a bed. Sid and I crawled in. There were cloths hung around the bed that hid us. We were too tired to appreciate we'd just completed our first day as escapees. We slept.

At dawn, we were awakened by the rattle of tin pans. We peeked out. A young girl who'd been milking a cow had brought the milk into the shed. Her back was turned to us. We watched silently, grinning to ourselves, saying nothing. I was on the side of the bed nearer the girl. I called loudly "Hallo!" The poor child heaved the pan filled with milk and fled. We snickered and lay back. Soon all members of the household were beside the bed, no doubt furious at our audacity and unsure whether we were friend or foe. They demanded an explanation. We tried to placate our reluctant hosts by displaying a few items we carried to identify ourselves. It was easy enough to achieve an understanding but not so easy to assuage their anger. They rather grudgingly asked us into the house. We had to go outside and enter the house through the only door of the small dwelling.

They offered us something less than a hearty breakfast. They might have been on short rations themselves. We produced the eggs we'd brought. Afterwards they permitted us use of the shed until it was dark enough for us to resume our walk toward Spain. We slept until about 4:00 p.m. and resumed our journey.

Our route now followed a narrow gauge railroad track. The track was straight and not difficult walking, but it was dangerous. It placed us much more in the open, and we were bound sooner or later to meet a train or walk into a railroad station. And so we did. Just before dawn we saw the lights of a small passenger depot. It was filled with Nazi soldiers. After observing them for a few minutes, we decided to try to walk right on by. It worked, and we passed unobserved. But daylight was coming.

The station was on the edge of a town, which we later learned was Mûr de Bretagne. We had no choice but to keep on walking, hoping to get through the town before it was full light and before anyone passed by. As we reached the eastern outskirts, we encountered people and managed to convince them we were the good guys—American airmen. We passed a cottage and the occupants saw us, knowing somehow we were not the enemy. Our clothing and gestures must have made that clear. It was a jolly old couple, fearless and at ease with the danger we posed for them. They told us to warm ourselves by the fireplace. We did. The old man offered us a glass of water, and I hastily took a large mouthful—but it was not water. It was *eau de vie*, as clear and colorless as water but as fiery as alcohol can get. I choked, coughed, but didn't spit on his floor. The onlookers—both the old man and his wife—laughed with delight at the joke they had played on their American friends.

A grandson appeared, a sturdy boy about thirteen or fourteen, and we were told that he would lead us to a chateau on the hill nearby. It is a vivid memory, walking in broad daylight up a long meadow, approaching a classic dwelling at the crown of the hill, towers buttressing each end. This was near St. Gilles Vieux Marche. Anyone looking toward that hillside meadow would have seen three men, an unusual sight in occupied France. That was a risk we had to take, one far more grave for the boy who would be left behind, vulnerable to the Nazi's clutches, than for the visitors who were passing through. Up the hill we trudged. At the chateau we found a side door and knocked on it. Our young guide introduced us to an old couple. Smiles burst upon their faces. Their arms opened. There was also, glory be, a beautiful young woman, a niece or granddaughter perhaps. She was Odile de Lavarenne, as well as I could translate what I heard. Again, we were fed. And, joy of joys, we were offered a hot bath, perhaps as much for our hosts' comfort as for our own.

Cleaned up and refreshed, we sat down with M. le Comte and Mme. la Comtesse de Keranflec, for that was the astonishing name of our astonishing hosts. (In Bretagne, the French language has ways of its own, ways unknown even to the sophisticated Parisians we would soon meet.) The count and countess were quite old, quite small, and very brave: "Do not look out the window of your tower room this afternoon," they ordered. "The Nazis are coming." The Keranflecs were playing a double game, and they would continue it through 1943 and 1944, having to give it up and flee in the final hours before Allied soldiers approached in June 1944. They did escape, and managed to return to their beautiful hilltop home, there to live happily ever after. The chateau was passed on to a descendant who hosted my wife, Mary Ann, and I on our first visit to Brittany in the summer of 1977.

They gave us a lovely room and English language novels to read. (As I recall, my novel was *Red Dust*, a romance.) They urged us to try to sleep until supper time. During this time we heard the sound of a motorcar pulling up. Sid and I shamefully disobeyed our hosts, peeking from a window in our third floor bedroom. We saw the Nazi staff car arrive, saw three officers knock at the front door and be admitted, saw them depart after a brief stay.

That evening, M. le Comte and Mme. la Comtesse sent for Sid and me. We convened in a large, high-ceilinged library. There we were given our instructions for the next morning. The family chauffeur, a brave young man who seemed to enjoy his part in this, would drive us to the rail station at Plaintel, a whistle stop a few miles away. Our hosts inspected the francs in our escape kits to ensure we had sufficient funds for our rail tickets. At Plaintel, they said, we would catch a train for St. Brieuc, a substantial town on the north coast of Brittany. There we would catch the Rapide, the express train, for Paris, arriving at the Gare du Nord after dark. How did these elderly Frenchmen manage to cheerfully risk their lives for the Allied cause, the cause of freedom, in the persons of Technical Sergeant Sidney Devers and Second Lieutenant John W.

Spence? Our diminutive host and hostess managed to demonstrate that courage does not necessarily depend on one's size. One might remember that the word *courage* derives from a French word, the word for heart: *coeur*.

The small car we crowded into the next morning with our cheerful chauffeur—interesting that cheer seemed to be everywhere at Chateau de Keranflec—was fueled by firewood. A bulky contraption called a Gasogen was mounted on the rear of the car to make it run. We putt-putted to the rail station where we nodded a discreet farewell to our driver.

The Keranflecs had given us clear, specific instructions about buying our rail tickets: what words to speak, that the stationmaster would be friendly, and that we soon would be on our way to friends living in Paris. Conjuring up my best French, I approached the uniformed stationmaster and issued my request. From my opening words it was clear that the stationmaster knew we were not French. He looked me in the eye, said nothing, gave me the tickets and my change, and then walked away.

Sid and I joined a queue to board the train. As it approached, the stationmaster walked directly toward me, not slowing down. I had no time to react. Bumping into me with his shoulder, he stopped.

"*Bon voyage!*" he whispered.

Those words lifted my heart. This was indeed a good omen.

A few minutes up the line, Sid and I stepped off our train and waited outside the station for the Rapide to Paris. Many German troops were also there. A freight train passed through the station. Behind it on flat cars were German antiaircraft guns, likely the type that only days ago had shot us down.

The Rapide pulled into the station on time and we stepped aboard. We were traveling third class. For seven hours, the train rode through the French countryside. We had been instructed to keep our mouths shut all the way, and we did. Fellow passengers showed little interest in the two peasants traveling to Paris.

We arrived after dark and took a Metro to the Gare du Nord. We went to the Military Red Cross station. "*Je suis américain,*" I said in my best French, as the Keranflecs had instructed, and asked for Mme. Suzanne Le Grand. Alas, the madam was not there. We identified ourselves by a picture of her grandnephew that had been provided us at the chateau. One of the women telephoned Mme. Le Grand, then offered to escort us herself. "I'll take you to St. Cloud," she said. "You'll never get there by yourself."

The three of us, Sid, me, and the Red Cross woman, boarded the train to St. Cloud. We got off and walked up the hill to the house at 4 avenue de Nancy, a walled, two-story house. There we were welcomed by Lady MacDonald Lucas, the French wife of an English nobleman. She was in her late middle years. Suzanne Le Grand was her married daughter. They both spoke English. There were no men present.

Sid and I remained inside for five days, not permitted outside the walls of the garden. One day Lady Lucas, thinking perhaps that in our boredom we might choose to go sightseeing, ordered us quite pleasantly to the cellar. There, she said, was a quantity of Irish potatoes. They were beginning to sprout, and that wouldn't do. We were to sit down and push the sprouts off every potato that had one. We did. It was a new chore and not hard to do. The following day we were allowed back into the garden.

One night a stranger came for dinner. She was introduced to us as an employee of the Irish embassy. For three or four hours the woman talked to us, no doubt attempting to verify our story. It was this woman who connected Lady Lucas to the Resistance and the members who arranged our flight from France. On our final day, the Irish lady delivered our doctored passports. I cherish a photograph Suzanne Le Grand took of the four of us: Lady Lucas, the lady from the Irish embassy, Sid, and I standing in the garden.

Many have asked how I was feeling during this time, hiding out in France amid Nazi soldiers all over the place. I wasn't as nervous as might be imagined. To appreciate why, consider this. When you have been in an airplane with its engines shot out by flak, and fighters pressing all around you and parachutes dropping, then hiding on the ground and running from the Nazis, you become calm. You think, "Man, I got this down pat." Fear was never with me after my parachute opened.

Arrangements were made for us to move on. Sid and I were sent to separate locations in the city, and we saw no more of each other until the night we left Paris. Soon we would be hiking over the Pyrenees Mountains to reach the safety of Spain. This would require no little amount of preparation, both on the part of our benefactors working in the Underground, and ourselves.

Eleanor Bonner Spence,
John's mother

John's father, John Wilson Spence

John's father (bottom row, third from left), with classmates, University of Tennessee, Knoxville, 1912

John's father, in the Philippines, as an officer overseeing a group of Philippine soldiers

*John's aunt (his father's sister),
Katie Belle Spence Conyers*

*John's godfather,
George Darrow, late 1920s*

John, riding in a goat-drawn cart, 1923

Spence and Huggins family members (standing, left to right: Jesse Huggins; Anne Bonner Huggins; Charles Kenneth Eves. Seated, left to right: Anne Spence; Lavinia Bonner Eves; Eleanor Bonner Spence; John; Lavinia "Granny" Murfree Burton)

John's sister, Anne Spence, in her early twenties

John, a second lieutenant in the Army Air Force

John, with Mary Binyon Wheeler on their wedding day, June 29, 1942,
Murfreesboro (in back are Anne Spence and Lawrence Eyerly)

John's sister Anne's wedding on June 30, 1942, Murfreesboro. Family members pictured left to right: Anne Bonner Huggins; Eleanor Bonner Spence; Mrs. Eyerly, mother of the groom; Jesse Huggins; Anne Spence Eyerly; Lawrence Eyerly; Mary Binyon Wheeler Spence; John; Lavinia Bonner Eves

Green Hornet and crew: back row, left to right: 1Lt Ellis J. Sanderson (P)(POW), 1Lt Horace D. Bowman (CP)(POW), 2Lt John W. Spence (M)(Evd), 2Lt John W. Plummer (B). Front row, left to right: T/Sgt Sidney Devers(E)(Evd), T/Sgt Miles B. Jones (R)(Evd), S/Sgt Harry F. Swanson(RWG)(POW); S/Sgt Frank W. Greene (BT)(Evd); S/Sgt Joseph L. Markiewicz (TG)(MIA). Not in photo: Sgt Carlos J Silva (LWG)(POW)

John in Paris in 1943 in the walled garden of 4 Avenue de Nancy, St. Cloud, Paris, late-January or early-February. From left: John; Lady McDonald Lucas; woman from the Irish embassy; T/Sgt. Sidney Devers. Photo taken by Suzanne Le Grand, daughter of Lady McDonald Lucas

Mary Ann Simonton, 1940s.

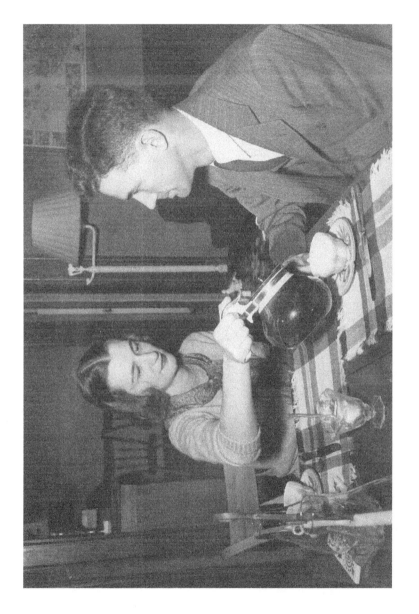

John, with Mary Ann Simonton Spence, Chattanooga, 1949

Newsman Reveals for First Time: He Was a Spy

Some Reflections on the Ethics of Espionage

By JOHN W. SPENCE
Press-Scimitar Staff Writer
(Formerly Captain,
United States Air Force)

Francis Gary Powers has been sentenced by the Russians to 10 years in prison.

The Germans, I think, might have done no worse to me had they caught me at a certain moment in France II years ago.

Millions of people the world over may be debating now the sentence imposed on Powers, just or unjust it may be. I do not propose to say, but I had an experience that may help them in their thinking.

So I'm offering to put in print for the first time the story of my own experience in World War II.

I signed a paper in London in 1943 saying I understood I was not to reveal for five years after the "cessation of hostilities" the things I had seen and done. Well, the five years is long past.

I was a spy.

Like Powers, I did not start out to be one. And, like Powers, I was shot down over enemy-occupied territory.

You may or may not think there are many similarities beyond those two. The important thing, I think, is what I learned of the attitudes and practices of the great powers in spying on one another. It was reassuring for Francis Gary Powers.

Here's the story:

On Jan. 23, 1943, a formation of United States Air Force Flying Fortresses attacked and bombed an enemy target at L'Orient, France. It was reported after the mission that "several of our aircraft are missing."

I was navigator on one of the missing planes. I arrived, still soil, by parachute, clad in bulky flying suit.

Within less than two hours, was wearing civilian clothes. Like Powers I carried a pistol. And like Powers. I spied. And I carried on my person the proof of my guilty photographs of value to my government in its war effort.

One of the persons who aided me in my weeks-long trip on foot and by train across 1000 miles or more of enemy-held and neutral territory was discovered by the Germans.

We believe he is dead. He has never been heard from since the Germans seized him and carried him away. He was a young Frenchman, a civilian.

The neutrals, the conquered, when they are caught co-operating with the enemy—seem almost always to be dealt with more severely than the "enemy" himself.

I am a graduate of MI-9. It was at MI-9 that I came to understand the attitudes of hostile powers to the agents of each other.

MI-9 was a British counter-intelligence school. The school was conducted in a handsome town house or small palace on the fringes of London, and the house had once been a summer residence of the Russian Czar, in the days when Russia had a Czar by that name.

At MI-9—after, and not before, my successful journey in civilian clothes among the Germans in France—I was in school with two score other men whose experiences were very much like mine.

We compared notes. We schooled one another in techniques of concealment, evasion, information-gathering. And our tutor was a veteran of such escapades in two wars.

The most impressive thing was that none of these men was a traitor. All spied not on their own countrymen but on other countries. And none really feared death at the hands of an enemy unless he were in the first tense moments of capture, or in an attempt at escape, or once captured.

As impressive was the nonchalant acceptance by all present of the idea that what they had done or might do again was commonplace.

To seek to discover what the enemy is doing is as natural not to want to be captured, I want no more chance to put on civilian clothes. I did.

When people offered me military intelligence, it would have been ungracious not to accept at least like mine.

And always, I believed that it would be obvious to my captors if I were caught that I was not very "professional" about my information-gathering—or spying.

The British did not shoot enemy aliens caught in efforts at espionage, so far as we knew. The Germans did not shoot those of us who were temporarily in their hands. There were men there at MI-9 who had been in Poland, in Austria, in Germany itself, in Italy.

As to what I did in France and why I did it: It was not of my own doing what others planned, and I only did what seemed sensible to do. I did was to spy on your own people.

John's "I was a spy" article, Memphis Press-Scimitar, 1961

John, a reporter for the Memphis Press-Scimitar *in the 1960s*

Southwestern Stages Protest March

The Sou'wester

Vol. 51, No. 23

Southwestern At Memphis

May 15, 1970

STRIKE

by Barbara Fowke

On Monday May 11, a march from Southwestern to the National Guard Armory was held to protest U.S. invasion of Cambodia and the killing of four Kent State students by National Guardsmen. The march left Southwestern about 1 p.m. with well over 200 people in the procession. Admittedly, not all of these were members of the Southwestern community, but the majority of them were.

For many of these people, participation in the march was the accompanied the students along the route. As well as newsmen, policemen were stationed along the McDonald's for assurance of hatched rules, police than walking

John in the anti-Vietnam War march at Southwestern, now Rhodes College, Memphis, 1970

Best Wishes
to John Spence

Jimmy Carter

John, as a member of the Tennessee group on the Democrats' National
Platform Committee, receiving greetings from President Jimmy Carter, at the
White House, 1980

John, in the 1980s

Chapter Eleven

Underground in Paris

On February 1, having had our bonafides checked, Sid and I departed the home of Lady Lucas and went our separate ways. I was assigned a guide by the name of Mr. Ayle. It was noon when we arrived at the home of Dr. George Tinel and his family. The apartment was located very near the Notre Dame Cathedral in the heart of the city. The address of their large, second floor apartment, 254 boulevard St. Germain, appeared on the side of the boulevard facing the Seine. Other occupants included Madame Tinel and their three grown children about my age: George, Jacques, and a daughter whose name I don't recall. I was given a pleasant room, high ceilinged with a tall window looking into a courtyard. It was not a room into which passers-by could see. The walls were lined with books.

I took my meals with the family, usually prepared and served by a small black woman. The food was plain but plentiful. There was wine also. Not everyone drank it, and those who did diluted it with water. The dining room overlooked the boulevard. On several days, the Nazi occupiers of Paris marched past in formation, sometimes halting for no apparent reason. The soldiers were well disciplined and responded precisely to command. I made the mistake of voicing admiration for their soldierly performance, drawing frowns and murmurs of disapproval from my hosts.

Despite the presence of the Nazis, George and Jacques began taking me for long walks through the streets of Paris soon after my arrival. George was pursuing medical studies and was less free than Jacques to take me on my daily walks. I saw much of central Paris. Mont St. Michel loomed in the north. The walks were not intended for our amusement, but rather to prepare me for the hike across the Pyrenees Mountains into Spain.

I never opened my mouth, a rule I followed anytime I stepped outside the Tinel home. My poor French would hardly suffice for public use. In the event I was stopped and questioned, I was instructed to identify myself with these words: "*Je suis Flamand marine*": that is, I was to be a Flemish sailor visiting Paris.

The weather was mild. There was little rain. My guides took me all over Paris: Notre Dame, Sacré Coeur, and even the legislative chambers. We did sometimes encounter Nazi soldiers; their uniforms, though neat, showed much wear. I was told these soldiers were veterans of the Eastern war against Russia. Duty in Paris, I suppose, was their reward for hard fighting. On one occasion a group of soldiers hailed us, asking directions, which Jacques easily supplied. On another occasion, we stopped in a café for coffee, or a coffee substitute. The place was filled with German soldiers, but they paid no attention to us. I never had to use my counterfeit passport.

At a nearby Paris department store, I acquired clothing far more suitable to the streets of Paris than my farm clothes. The few thousand francs I'd carried in my escape kit were nowhere near enough to buy what my hosts thought I needed, so they generously provided the twenty thousand francs for a handsome, well fitting suit, one I wore proudly many years later in the United States.

One evening, Jacques took me to a large, three-story apartment building surrounding a courtyard. Located at 61 rue de Varenne, the apartment housed the sisters Henriette and Genevieve, women our own age whose parents had moved to the South of France because they had Jewish blood. We'd come to pay them a visit because they'd expressed an interest in the Allied airmen. Hosting us was a very risky activity with no purpose other than to demonstrate the gratitude many Parisians felt toward the Allies. One of the sisters, Genevieve, volunteered to be my escort on several afternoon walks.

For security purposes—to prevent my benefactors' identity from somehow being leaked to the Germans—I was never told the sisters' last names. Nor did they know mine. Everything was done on a first-name-only basis. One evening after a typically long walk—including, thankfully, a supper outside the Tinels' home—Genevieve dropped me off at the Tinel residence. As I began to mount the stairs, I turned to her. Normally I would say "*bon soir*," and she the same. This night I was feeling reckless. "John Spence," I said. Her face lit up, having received this most illicit and dangerous revelation. Her one-word reply: "Noufflard." I committed it to memory. This recklessness later enabled Genevieve to locate me in the United States once the war was over. Years later, I learned that Jacques was caught by the Nazis and perhaps tortured before he was executed. The older son George survived.

Visits by the woman from the Irish embassy continued. She would question me about life in America. It was obvious that her purpose was to make sure I was not a Nazi infiltrator. One day she began asking questions about baseball. Every red-blooded American should know about baseball. But this one did not. Were I to fail a test, would I be led away for execution? Later another interrogator, this time a man known only to me as Mr. B., came to quiz me. He was an Englishman and he said he was trying to learn for himself better ways of identifying Americans. I was not convinced that this was his only purpose.

It was Mr. B. who came for me on the Saturday night of my planned departure to Spain. As my interrogator led me through the dark streets of wartime Paris, supposedly taking me to the station, I wondered whether I would survive this night. I sighed mightily with relief when we finally entered the well-lit station.

My helpers had done a brilliant job of planning the coming journey. Mr. B. furnished first-class tickets. Five others joined me, filling the compartment and thus precluding the unwelcome company of any other passengers. Here I was reunited with my crewmember and fellow escapee Sid Devers. The others were Sergeant Harry Chastain, a Royal Canadian Air Force pilot, and three French-speaking escorts, one for each one of us. They were either Belgian or British-born Frenchmen—not a native among us.

We each had tickets to Bayonne, France, but on Sunday morning we disembarked early at Dax, a small town in the far south. There we spent the day along with many French people enjoying a Sunday excursion. One pastime in the village was watching games of *boules* played outdoors on the turf. We lunched pleasantly and attended an afternoon movie. A Nazi soldier on his holiday sat beside me in the movie house. By now I'd become accustomed to hiding behind my Flemish disguise, though no words were exchanged.

That evening we caught the local train to Bayonne—but again, at an intermediate stop, we left the train. This time we walked a few steps along the platform, then transferred to yet another train which pulled out of the station almost immediately. Our train chugged up the mountains on a precipitous cliff side that overlooked a beautiful stream. At dusk our guides pulled a cord and stopped the train. We left it to go directly onto a swinging footbridge over the stream.

Chapter Twelve

Flight

It was nearly dark when we crossed the swinging footbridge. A full moon hung low in the cold sky, casting shadows across the way. One of the shadows moved. It was the Basque guide awaiting our arrival. Seven silent figures now walked single file through the night. No one spoke. Ahead loomed a boulder, which moved and became our relief guide. An hour later another guide appeared. Up into the hills we continued, until we reached a farmhouse where we were expected. We entered a warm, brightly lit room full of men. There was food. We turned over our false passports; they would be needed for the next group of escapees. We put on some blue cotton trousers.

Soon we were traversing a cliff top, led by a new guide who traveled with us for many hours. He wore frail street shoes, soon shredded by the rocks. But he was dauntless. Ever faithful to his duty, he would whisper, "*Attention! Attention!*" It sounded more like a groan than a caution, but he was doing his best to help his fellow travelers. I couldn't help smiling to myself in the dark, but I am infinitely grateful to him and the others. Sometime in the early morning hours, we reached the frontier and crossed it. We were now in Spain.

Not long after, our guides informed us that they were leaving, heading off to the city of San Sebastian. They gave us easy-to-follow directions to our next stopping point. At 4:30 a.m., we stopped at a farmhouse for food and a short rest. We hiked on. Three hours later we arrived at a second farmhouse. Here we were fed and put to bed.

That evening we three airmen made our way down the mountain.

With the confidence born of having escaped the Nazis, we sauntered onto the main street of a small town, Elizando. We'd practically arrived home, or so we thought. It was foolish of us, I suppose, walking into the main street of a village. Spanish dictator Franco had avoided going to war, but many there felt Hitler to be an ally. Spain resisted any appearance of supporting the Allies. The Spanish police, *Guardia Civil*, would have none of our behavior. They arrested us, searched us, and marched us off to headquarters. We crowded the small space. We were ordered to empty our pockets. They examined what we had, then gave it back to us. Then we started a march to the jail.

The most dangerous moments of my whole escape from France came then: guards wearing handsome, large capes led us to the dungeon. Should I try to make a break? Coward that I am, I decided not to do it. And I was very glad a moment later at the prison gates. The guards threw back their handsome capes in order to open the jail door, revealing cocked pistols in their hands.

Huge doors opened, and inside were stone walls. The prison was medieval. Our cell, quite large, had no light. No heat. No chairs. There was a barred window with no glass, open to the weather, and it was still winter. A steep sloped platform was to be our bed for the night. There were no covers to protect us from the cold. We were locked in for the night, or the week, or the month. There was no way to know.

We slept fitfully. Soon after daylight, our jailer appeared at the window. Sergeant Chastain spoke Spanish. Our jailer was friendly toward the Allies, he told us. He related cheerfully that the Nazis had been turned back at Stalingrad. The guard and Chastain conferred. Did we have money, the guard asked? Would we pay for a taxi to take us thirty or forty kilometers up and downhill to Pamplona? Would we pay the fare for as many of our captors as could crowd into the creaky old Citroen?

It was a deal. Seven grown men crowded into the car and headed for Pamplona. The car began to break down. The clattering engine sounded as if it would surely not get us there. We looked at each other, grinned, and held our breath. We clanked into town.

Members of our police escort thanked us for the ride and bade us good-bye, leaving us in the hands of officials who were fluent in English. We three airmen were interrogated separately. Sid and Sarge Chastain knew not what I was saying, and I did not know what they were telling their interrogator. I had been coached back in England. I knew the right stories to tell: I was a Royal Air Force officer. I had a home in London. The Nazis had captured me, but I had escaped. This lie was important. We'd been taught that evadees such as myself—those who had escaped capture altogether—received harsher treatment than POW escapees. This was because it was assumed we would have had help from the underground resistance (which is exactly what happened); we might have been tortured to reveal what we knew.

Assuming the name and rank British Flying Officer Spence, I was sent on my way to the plush quarters of the Hotel Maisonave, though I was still under guard. A husband and wife ran the place. Three lovely young brunette women—Engracia, Eleana, and Emilia—waited tables. The food was fine. The other two, both having admitted to be North Americans, went to an uncomfortable jail not unlike our quarters in the little border town. We would come together a couple of weeks later to ride in a British Embassy car to Madrid. At the hotel, I joined about thirty other officers—Belgian, French, American. They comprised a remarkable group. Some had made their way hundreds of miles from Nazi prisons in East Germany. They chose to hold a session each morning at which they would lecture the group on their specialties, or their experiences in escaping. Some were tank officers, other infantry. I attended the sessions.

By now it was late February, and the weather was mild. Many afternoons, a guard would accompany the group on a long and pleasant walk. We developed an honor system. We would not try to escape if we were allowed to roam the town.

Pamplona was a medieval, hilltop town nearly surrounded by a clear, swift stream. Spanish women washing their clothes in the river was a lovely sight. The laundresses had a way of throwing a bed sheet out over the water so that it fell wide open. Then, after it filled with water and slowly sank, they would pull it back.

I shared a bedroom with Charles Maindel, a Belgian officer who proved to be a quiet and considerate roommate. We all shared a single shower on our floor, probably the only one in the hotel. A shower cost us extra.

As a purported British officer, my credit was good, though in reality I was an American to the hoteliers. The British officers who interrogated me were glad to carry on the notion that I was one of them, the better to serve their American comrade. There were two other Americans at the hotel. They had arrived before me, and they were there after I left. My American companions chose to drink a good deal of wine with their meals. The U.S. government later explained to them that *they* would pay for their wine and their meals. My British bosses paid for mine.

Two weeks passed. One morning a big British car, a Humber—similar to an American Buick—came to get me. We drove to the jail and picked up poor Sid Devers and Chastain. The drive south to Madrid was as pleasant as could be, and included a midday stop for an excellent lunch. By nightfall we were delivered to the British Embassy. There we were housed somewhat less elegantly than we might have hoped, but very comfortably in a building on the embassy grounds. We stayed about four or five days. One evening we were told to get in a staff car, and we were taken somewhere in Madrid where we joined a room full of men. A tall, blond, "veddy veddy" British fellow took charge of us, and we headed for the station.

On the train I slept most of the way. In the morning we were in the south of Spain, and I observed a bit sadly that the countryside was not so well kept as in the north. As a native Southerner, I saw how much it resembled the American South.

At midday, we reached Gibraltar. An American officer, a middle-aged colonel of coast artillery, took charge. To my surprise, as we lined up for inspection, our "British" escort fell in with the rest of us—he was not British at all, he was a Dutchman.

My host, the Dutch colonel, expressed discomfort with my lack of a uniform. American uniforms were not to be found on Gibraltar in the spring of 1943, so the colonel insisted that I don a British one. This suited me fine. My companions, when I found some, were British navy officers who were pleased to get acquainted with a Yank.

I wandered freely over the hilltop where the American quarters were. I was pretty much by myself. I could see across the straits to the African coast. Gazing out over the Mediterranean, I felt a weight lifting from my shoulders. I'd proven myself by doing something real and more meaningful than all the Scout merit badges in the book. Shedding the heavy armor of privilege, I'd moved quickly to evade capture. I realized when I returned home to Memphis, I would be ready for anything. I could be anyone I chose to be.

The next day Sid and I departed from Spain. We were bound for England and home. Miles of Nazi-infested ocean remained to be crossed.

Chapter Thirteen

London

Sid and I boarded the troopship *Letitia* headed for Scotland. Escorted by two destroyers, she was part of a British convoy of ten ships. We were thrilled we'd managed to escape the Nazis, but the truth was they were still hunting people like us—only this time at sea. We had to reach friendly shores before we could fully relax. Ships in our convoy had guns for defense against air attack, and all on board were expected to take turns manning them. I manned my station several times, but never saw a Nazi plane. The airplanes we did see were presumably our protectors. Our escorts seemed to sense Nazi subs, especially at mealtimes below decks when we often heard—and felt—the rumble of underwater depth charges being dropped on the hidden enemy.

The officer/enlisted-man hierarchy prevailing, Sid went to a deck one below mine. We also dined separately. The officers' mess served the best food I tasted during the war. It consisted of five elegantly served courses. One of my tablemates was an RAF pilot who had defended Malta. His uniform was worn and ragged, but he was a proud soldier and quite at ease.

We were at sea for ten days, observing the color of sea and sky change each day as we sailed north. One night, a ship in our convoy disappeared. I never learned whether it fell behind or whether it was torpedoed and sunk. On April 15, we docked at Glasgow. No one aboard seemed to think they had any responsibility for Sid and me. We found a military advisor who provided us tickets for a London-bound train, and we boarded it that same day.

Fresh off the transport ship, I realized that four months had passed since I'd last set foot in the off-duty paradise of London. This time there was no one to receive us. I suppose I was hoping for some kind of welcoming committee, but there were only strangers on the streets. With no official recognition, we were free to go where we pleased. Sid headed for his favorite watering hole, a noncommissioned officers' club he had visited in the days before we were shot down. I checked into the Jules Officers' Club in Jermyn Street. I looked up my girlfriend Inga, and found out she had gotten herself another fellow.

Finally we reported to the Supreme Headquarters, Allied Forces Europe. No one there had any ideas for us, not even offering us transport back to RAF Molesworth. After a day or two, someone thought these odd birds had better be corralled and interrogated. We were more or less confined in a hotel that served as quarters for military personnel. Interrogators wanted to know if I was a German trying to infiltrate the British Empire. They brought down a couple of U.S. Intelligence officers from Molesworth. These were a Major Nelson and a first lieutenant whose name I no longer remember. Both were men I liked. Nelson, in his fifties I think, was from the family that owned the *Kansas City Star*. My lieutenant, a fellow in his late thirties or early forties, was a good-natured, easy-going fellow—and a member of my 303rd bomb group. He was able to look me in the eye, hear my voice, and say, "Yes, that's John Spence."

Since the day we'd been shot down, there'd been no way to communicate with my wife or the rest of my family. Now that I was back behind Allied lines, official communication from the Adjunct General was wired to the U.S. By then, Weetsie was living with my mother in Memphis. The first words they'd received about our ill-fated flight—that we were missing in action—had come a couple of days after January 23. Now another telegram was sent after I was back in London being interrogated. It said Lt. John W.

Spence returned to active duty on such and such a date. Our communication was crude. I don't recall whether there was radio communication from England to the States, or whether I had the opportunity to send a telegram myself.

My two U.S. shepherds stayed with me through the interrogations. Following the preliminary interviews, the RAF sent an unlikely official to guide me to its official inquisitors. British Flying Officer Veronica K. Berry turned out to be a tall and beautiful blonde woman, hardly more than a girl despite her several years as a WAAF, or Women's Auxiliary Air Force. V. K. Berry immediately suggested that we Americans call her Nicky, short for Veronica. It was rare that all three escorts were with me; often it was just one. And naturally enough, it was the most fun when it was just Nicky and me.

Veronica Katherine Berry had been in uniform since early in the war. We dined together often, and attended the London theater. There was a wedding ring on my third finger, left hand, and it never left that finger. But it couldn't prevent a strong affection, a love affair, budding between Nicky and me. We decided one evening to spend the night at Grosvenor House, then one of London's best hotels. (U.S. Air Force flying officers were probably the best-paid soldiers in England.) We went to bed. We kissed and enfolded each other in our arms. We shed most of our clothes. But then Nicky's scruples asserted themselves. We came very close, but something persuaded her to tell me, tearfully, that she just couldn't do it. I think she was not a virgin. I liked and respected her way too much to be angry with her, and we slept like a couple of puppies. We woke on Sunday morning to take the train to Kent to meet her mother and father. I remember it all so happily. The train ride took an hour or so. It was a gorgeous, sunny spring day. If Nicky had made any explanations to her folks—probably she had phoned them the day before—she hadn't told me about it. They welcomed the American airman with genuine warmth and served a Sunday dinner. Then we took the train back to London.

We never saw each other again. Why didn't we swap letters, keep in touch? One obvious reason is that I was married. You may wonder why I didn't worry more about any of the relationships I had with English women, but it was wartime, and the conventions seemed to be somewhat different. Fifty-eight years later I don't know that I was wrong, very wrong anyway, to enjoy the warm welcome I was given. Once I had departed the States I had felt little attachment to Weetsie, to anyone—not even my crewmates on whom my life depended. I was caught up in the war. My life now belonged to the Army Air Force. If I had any authorship, it was only in momentary events. In the sky, I aimed my machine gun and kept track of our position. On the ground, I aimed for sources of comfort and rest. There was no concept of future. The future did not exist. That included everyone I knew back home: my mother, my friends, my wife.

After a short stay at Molesworth I, along with other fellow escapees and evaders, was sent to a school called MI9, which stood for Military Intelligence 9. The school was located in a palace, a grand home on the outskirts of London. There we shared our experiences with each other. I recall everyone else's to be more exciting and dangerous than mine.

I was still a second lieutenant and was mad about that. Most of my colleagues had received their promotion to first lieutenant. One old officer took me aside. He said, "Don't let yourself be bitter." I received my promotion shortly before I left for home.

During my final days in London, I was assigned to the job of morale building. With an assigned staff car and a driver, I went all around telling what a fun thing it was to get shot down. By the time of my return to England, the Eighth Bombardment Command had been elevated to the Eighth Air Force. We were rapidly building the powerful armada that would soon send a thousand planes deep into Germany. But we had suffered dreadful casualties, and would continue to do so. The mere sight of me standing before the new airmen, and their hearing my message of survival, was meant to improve morale. I told about the joys of avoiding capture and being cared for by the French Resistance. And about our easy crossing of the Pyrenees. I was chosen for this assignment because I was surely one of the most fortunate ones to be shot down, having been able to evade the Nazis. (I was tallied as Evadee No. 16. I recall one fellow, Gilbert Showalter from Milwaukee, very proud of Milwaukee beer, also made it back. He was Evadee No. 15.) I told my fellow fliers that being one of the very great number of us who became "missing in action" did not have to mean that one was dead, wounded, or captured.

The Air Force had good cause for concern. There were times, following a succession of missions with very high losses, when it seemed that no one would finish twenty-five missions and make it home to the States. Of the thirty-five crews that crossed the North Atlantic the October night I did, only eight crews survived intact. The Eighth Air Force lost thirty-six thousand men before VE Day in April 1945.

Chapter Fourteen

Return to the States

My tour complete, I was sent back to the States in a chartered Pan American seaplane. The flight took seven days. We followed the perimeter of the Atlantic Ocean the long way around. We flew first to the west of England, then to Ireland; from Ireland to Portugal, then to a Portuguese colony on Africa's west coast. There we spent a late afternoon and night on an inland lake in Liberia, deep in the jungle. During our stopover I walked alone into a silent African village as far as time permitted, catching glimpses of shy natives who were catching glimpses of me.

I have an 8-by-10–inch certificate from Pan American Airways System that attests: "…John W. Spence on this 15th day of May in the 40th year (flying time) was borne on the wings of an airliner of the Pan American Airways System across the Equator en route from Africa to Brazil." The certificate states that we "crossed the equator at 0010 hours at altitude 8000 feet/ Air Speed 115 mph. Weather Good."

Flying across the Atlantic from Africa, we landed near the Brazilian town Belem on the banks of the Amazon River. We tied up in the vast river's mouth, and I could almost hear it emptying into the Atlantic Ocean. We spent about twenty-four hours in Belem, and again I was free to roam. But the streets seemed deserted. On the continued flight north we made several stops, arriving in New York City in mid May. My aunt, Lavinia Bonner Eves, and her husband, Charles Kenneth Eves, met me at LaGuardia. I flew on to Memphis as fast as I could.

On my first night home with Weetsie, hours after our reunion, when we were in bed and had had sex, Weetsie surprised me—I should not have been surprised—by asking, "Were you faithful to me?" I answered: "No." She was quiet and we went to sleep, and not another word was ever spoken about that.

When I returned to the States, I said, "The war is over for me," but I didn't really know. Some people who got shot down and escaped might have gone back into combat. But because part of my means of escape out of France was in civilian clothes, the Germans could assume I had gotten out *by not wearing my uniform.* As soon as a soldier gets out of uniform, he is termed a spy—and the Germans made it a practice of shooting on sight airmen not in uniform. This was a problem for POWs and downed airmen: they had to stay in uniform or they would be shot as spies. But staying *in* uniform made it hard to escape at all. So the Germans now considered me a spy.

Following a few days' leave in Memphis with my wife, I was given some assignments. I worked for a few days outside of Washington in a secluded office used for intelligence purposes. I flew to many airbases in the southeastern United States giving the same lectures I'd given in England.

I bought a 1940 Pontiac sedan, a navy blue car, a straight-eight; that is, eight cylinders in-line. It was a fine car, not so expensive then as cars made a year or so later when the period of no civilian production made passenger cars scarcer. It was a great car. I drove it to Weetsie's parents' home in Eutaw, Alabama while she was visiting with her parents. Weetsie enjoyed driving the Pontiac. She looked good in it. She looked good in everything.

During those few months, Weetsie had a job with a Memphis airline, either Braniff or its predecessor. Soon she quit her job and went with me by train to Salt Lake City, Utah. I have a photo of a weary Weetsie, who had just finished a hike with me up the mountainside from the city. It may have been then in Utah that Weetsie got pregnant. We lost the child in July at the Gartly-Ramsay hospital in Memphis.

Somehow I found out that our tail gunner, Staff Sergeant Markiewicz, had been so badly wounded when we were shot down that he had died in a hospital a few days later, our only fatality.

I never saw Sid Devers again. I didn't write to him and he never wrote to me. I'm not proud of the way I behaved then. I just didn't have a realization about what was happening. I did, however, have a reunion with my pilot, Sandy Sanderson, which was arranged. I went down to Miami Beach to see him in August of 1945.

Sandy had been a prisoner in a German POW camp since the day our plane went down. He didn't talk much about his POW experience. He was not a wordy fellow. He was phlegmatic, pleasant, mostly a smiling guy, a Midwesterner.

He did tell me about the final minutes of our ill-fated flight. He and his copilot Dale both carried chest packs for parachutes. These snapped on easily, and so they were usually set aside during the flight and not worn. I don't know when these two thought they were going to have a chance to put them on. Normally, when the first person goes out the forward hatch, the open exit leaves a hole that's going to stay there forever. A loose parachute can easily bounce out of that hole, which is what probably happened to one of the two chest packs. So there they were, Sandy and Dale, their airplane going down and only one parachute between them. Each one was saying to the other: "You take it." Neither one was willing to take the parachute. They both said, "Shucks, we'll take the ship down together." And they did. They did a fine job of it. In the crash landing, Sandy lost a finger. Dale had some injuries, from which he fully recovered. They were both held prisoner until the end of the war. I've never seen Sandy since.

The Cross at Sewanee had been erected after World War I as a memorial to the local boys who served in or lost their lives in World War I. I sometimes wonder if that cross might have cast a curse on us Sewanee boys:

about half my 1935 SMA classmates were casualties in World War II. Having graduated from a military school and, in many cases, having gone on to college at a military school, we were perfect cannon fodder. We went straight into service as second lieutenants. Years later, on a return to the Mountain, I saw my war's toll inscribed on a wall.

My Faxon Avenue friends, Herbert (Buddy) Morris Jr., Fred Fiedler Jr., Burch Williams, Jimmy Humphreys, Bud Gowan, and Jack Orbison were all killed or wounded. Fred and Buddy, my closest friends on Faxon, were killed in the last days of the war in Europe. Fred was also an officer; I'm not sure what service he was in. As kids we'd played football in his backyard three doors up the street. Buddy, whose two-story clubhouse was the site of our 1930 Armistice Day celebration, became a captain in the infantry before he was killed. Burch Williams suffered some casualty but survived. We had been ripe for action. None of us had any inkling of our fate. Today, as an old man, I think with anger about the stupidity of war and of the behaviors—our behaviors—that get us into wars.

Saddest of all was the loss of my Sewanee roommate and close friend Jimmy Powell. He and I had gone our separate ways. He learned to fly in civilian life and became a Marine Corps pilot during the war. He was killed flying a Corsair fighter plane in the Pacific. No one was sure exactly what happened. He was an ace. As I heard it, while I was in my own war 10,000 miles away, he was flying with other planes out over the Pacific Ocean. He'd just shot down four Japanese planes. On the return flight he slid out of the formation and hit the sea. I don't know if there was a Japanese plane that just came in and made a lucky hit. But that was the end of Jimmy.

I've grown old with this mystery about Jimmy. Those smarter people who asked themselves what happened never came up with an answer, none that I know of. But I've never stopped wondering. In recent years I think I've come up with the answer. Knowing Jimmy as I did, I believe that he became sickened with the notion of slaughtering more Japanese, as he no doubt would be expected to continue doing. And on this last mission, having sent four of his fellow warriors into the deep, he may easily have decided to follow them to their graves. Of course I have no proof of this, but it's what I think happened.

In early June, 1943, I was assigned to the 469th Air Force base in Alexandria, Louisiana. That was a bitter arrival. Alexandria was overcrowded with camps and bases. The sight of a soldier was not a joy to anyone down there, except for the people making money from us. Weetsie and I checked in at the main hotel and spent a night there. We had to shuffle around to find some private accommodations. A delightful, kind Catholic family, the Jordons, took pity on us and invited us into their home with their six or seven children. We stayed there until we were given base quarters, which were very nice. They were small duplexes, operated under all kinds of regulations—which we immediately violated by getting a dog. We were a month or two or three in these nice quarters. But we wanted a dog. And so we got Angus, or Gus, as we called him. He was a purebred Scottish terrier puppy. They kicked us out. "You can't have a dog here."

We moved on, arriving at the back bedroom of a family named Els. Mr. Els made his living as a baker. We had a kitchen, a bedroom, and a bath, and that was it. It wasn't the greatest accommodation. But we had the big old Pontiac. I could come home every night from the base.

We were training replacement crews. We did a splendid job. Most of the airmen were veterans from the Pacific. They didn't know about the air war in Germany, but they knew about flying planes and shooting guns. My job after a while shifted over to celestial navigation. I worked hard as an instructor of crews. I was temporarily assigned to Chanute Field, Illinois, where I learned to instruct in an air-conditioned, darkened tower made to resemble the night sky. A fellow from the Missouri boot heel, Ben Leis, I think, and Art Sherman and Ramah E. Maidment were my fellow instructors.

In the spring of 1944, I learned I was entitled to R&R, to go somewhere to recuperate from the ardors of war—an unexpected perk which, as a virtual newlywed with an easy job, I didn't anymore need than the man in the moon. However, I wasn't about to pass it up. Weetsie and I were authorized gasoline to drive the Pontiac from Louisiana to Castle Hot Springs, Arizona. It was located in a desert ravine about seventy miles north of Phoenix. We suffered a bumpy ride getting there, but it proved to be a pleasant excursion. We stayed a month, riding horseback, playing tennis, reading about life in the Southwest from a very good private library. We ate well-prepared food. It was a place where the Rockefellers and Vanderbilts had stayed. As a patriotic gesture, the owners had said to the government, "Take it and use it." Castle Hot Springs was a Shangri-La. We stayed our allotted time, then came back home to Louisiana.

In the fall, Weetsie conceived again. In the spring of 1945, she was about six months pregnant. We were thinking of the war's end, of perhaps my seeking a job in journalism in California, of the birth of the child. We were still in our apartment in the baker's house, still driving our 1940 Pontiac. We were happy. I was teaching navigation to young airmen whose next stops would be combat stations in the war theaters, as the wars continued. The war in Europe seemed almost over, but the Japanese, as far as most of us knew, might fight on for a long time. It was a rainy April. We lived our usual lives, working each day, going to the Officers' Club to dance and be with our friends on weekends. Weetsie had the car when she wanted it, taking me to and from the air force base a few miles out of town when I could not catch a ride with a fellow worker. All seemed well.

One day Weetsie said she wasn't feeling well, that she had stomach pains and a cold. Soon she was in the Alexandria hospital. She had a doctor she liked, a kind, young man. Then it was pneumonia. It rained each day, seeming to rain all day. It was dreary. April 12 came. No different from the days before. Or so we thought. Then Weetsie lost consciousness.

Her doctor sat beside the bed. I stood on the other side. The doctor said, "Her heart has failed." His anguish was plain. "Do you want me to try to save the child?" I suppose I should have tried to shove the decision back to him. Or asked him to say what the chances were: a six-month fetus in 1945? That was a long time ago. I still do not know whether my answer was right. I said no. I think my answer was wrong.

Franklin Delano Roosevelt also died that day, April 12, 1945. The nation mourned a great and beloved man. I mourned a twenty-four-year-old girl. Besides her husband, she left her parents, Mr. and Mrs. J. W. Wheeler, and a brother, J. W. Wheeler Jr.

Weetsie had not wanted her mother to know of her pregnancy yet. I had not tried to change her mind. Mrs. Wheeler had not even known that her daughter was ill, so brief it was, with such an unexpected outcome. It was I, of course, who telephoned the shocking, heart-breaking, inexplicable news to Eutaw. I agreed to bury Weetsie there. The service was held in the little Episcopal Church in Eutaw where Weetsie and her family were members. There was, briefly and inevitably, an open casket. Mrs. Wheeler looked at her daughter's face, then at the part of her slender body visible in the casket. "Why is her body so swollen?" Mrs. Wheeler exclaimed in dismay and bewilderment. She was never to know.

Eutaw, though a county seat, was a tiny town with no cemetery of its own, so Weetsie's body lies today in a cemetery a few miles away. I chose the gravestone, a fairly massive, low granite one. It was a tombstone for two, her name and birth and death dates on one side, room beside it for John W. Spence's dates.

MARY BINYON WHEELER
WIFE OF
JOHN WILSON SPENCE
1920—1945

Part III

On My Feet

Chapter Fifteen

Cub Reporter

Several months of uncertainty unfolded after Weetsie's death. We airmen were not sure whether we would have to continue bombing Japan in order to end the war. Some, including me, having already fought the air war in Europe, felt sure that for us the war was over. I returned to my instructing job at the Alexandria Air Force Base, in Louisiana, and I did a lot of flying around the United States during those months. Without a family, I was required to move back onto the base, where I occupied a stark, barren, partly private room in a one-story frame building. I had sold the Pontiac. After Weetsie's death I just didn't feel like driving it anymore.

Then in the summer of 1945, American soldiers, sailors, and airmen were told we could leave the service. Or stay. Millions seized their chance to go back to civilian life. I was one, though I had no real plans for the future. I had supposed naively, or foolishly, that there would be a job in civil aviation for me. But with the postwar glut of pilots, airlines offered jobs such as forty dollars a week for sweeping out the office.

One evening I made a call to Boston. A sleepy and irritated Genevieve Noufflard seemed reluctant to accept the late night call. She ought not to have been; it was she who had set the wheels in motion, trying to renew contact with the Allied airman whom she and her sister Henriette had dared to invite to tea in Nazi-occupied Paris. Her government had recently sent her to the United States to tell Americans that many of the people of France had done what they could to resist the Nazis. I flew to New York City, meeting her there. My New

York aunt and uncle put us up. Genevieve and I spent a lot of time together; I remember a boat trip around Manhattan, and a visit to a theater as the reluctant guest of some older man who had some connection to Genevieve. I think Genevieve fell in love with me then. My feeling for her was strong, but perhaps it was not love.

In September, I returned to Memphis, where I temporarily moved into my old room at 1422 Faxon Ave. My mother had continued her career in education, and was now the principal of St. Paul's School. I was restless and looking for work. One day she said to me: "One of my teachers is sick. Come over and be a substitute teacher." That was a hilarious and, fortunately, a very brief experience. I didn't yet know how to handle little children. It was a classroom that, if I'd stayed long enough, I'd have had to teach five or six different things. Nonetheless, that experience might have contributed to my desire to teach, an interest I would take up as a career in years to come.

More seriously, I started to turn toward journalism. I'd made up my mind while I was in the Air Force that, barring a job in aviation, I wanted to get into journalism. Perhaps it was my experience in the Boy Scouts as the troop scribe. Or it might have been the meticulous record keeping involved with navigating using star sights and mathematical calculations. So I set out to build a civilian career: a day or two after the teaching fiasco, I went to the U.S. Employment Service and asked for a job in journalism. I said I wanted to be a newspaper reporter. The next day a woman from the Employment Service called with an offer of an interview at the Covington *Leader*, a large and respected weekly forty miles north of Memphis in the Tipton County seat. I dressed in a handsome tan summer suit, an extravagance acquired just before the war, and went up for my interview.

I was pretty cocky. I would not have cared greatly if I had not gotten a job there. I knew nothing about Covington or the owners of the paper. The *Leader* occupied a one-story storefront on South Main a few steps off the Square.

Upon entering, one faced a chest-high counter. Behind it sat two attractive young women and perhaps a middle-aged man or two. The dark-haired receptionist turned out to be the publisher's daughter, Mary Ann Simonton. Her father, Mr. Alison Simonton, whom I would always call Mr. Alison, interviewed me. He introduced me to his brother, known as Mr. Billy, who helped run the paper. Two other brothers whom I met later served as absentee owners.

I don't remember Mr. Alison's questions. Surely they concerned my education, my ability to write, to type. It occurs to me now that although Mr. Alison must have hired a good many people in his more than twenty-five years at the paper, he might have been ever so slightly impressed by the well-dressed, college educated, just retired Air Force captain who had flown in bombers against the Germans in Europe. Maybe a little; but not much.

The question of pay came up. I had been taking home the then princely sum of about $440 a month. I was now offered $40 a week. Whatever I said brought this rejoinder: "If you aren't worth more soon, you won't stay." I took it. I may have gone home to Memphis, told my mother, conveyed my thanks to the Employment Service woman, and returned to Covington the next day to start work.

I took a room a block or so down South Main at Miss Willie Clark's boarding house. I shared it with a very pleasant recruiting solider. The house was just across the street from the Simonton home at 532 South Main, which was almost exactly like the house at 404 Main in Murfreesboro where I was born.

I did all forms of journalism work: writing editorials, walking the street to gather news, proofreading all copy. My first big story turned out to be the Japanese surrender aboard the battleship *Missouri* on September 2, 1945. I obtained most of the material from the Memphis *Commercial Appeal*, which had few subscribers in our rural area. One regular story I developed on my own was a report from the retailers on the Square about their ups and downs. I thought I was right clever because I overcame the retailers' fears of letting their competition know too much. I did this by allowing them anonymity and always having a least three sources on hand. That way, no one could ever be exactly sure who the quoted source was.

I also covered fires. The fire station was next door to the *Leader* office. Most firemen were volunteers who came running when the siren sounded. I would dash out the door to meet them, coattails flying, and jump onto the rear of the fire engine. The girls in the office thought that was very exciting. I did too. Farm news was also a big thing, and the county agent, Wayne McGowan, valued all the coverage we would give it. I was fond of Mr. McGowan, although I recognized his cynicism and job weariness. We had tragedies to report sometimes. A young boy's drowning in a farm pond near town was one of them.

The women in the office took care of society news: the weddings, the parties, the comings and goings. Anyone who could read and spell helped edit the "County Correspondence." This was an important part of the paper. We tried to find a person, most often a woman, in every hamlet in the county to mail in every scrap of news she could gather.

Whenever a customer came in with a want ad, or classified ad, whoever was in the office was expected to accept it, take the money, and place the ad. One of my classic boners was the man who wanted to sell his pigs. It came out in the paper, thanks to me, as: "For sale: 5,000 pigs." I was supposed to have heard: "Five sows and pigs." Everybody in the office greatly enjoyed this city slicker's show of ignorance.

Soon I was called the editor of the paper. I wrote the editorials, edited almost all the copy, selected items for coverage, and fixed their placement. I was also a proofreader of both news and ads. Proofreading was actually a two-person job. One read aloud while the other "followed copy"—that is, saw that the reader was in fact reading what the advertiser wanted to advertise. I think that

Mr. Alison always read my editorials before sending them back to the linotype operators. Very rarely did we disagree. At least once, however, when Mr. Alison thought I had gone too far, we had to hash it out, preserving mutual respect.

It should be known that Mr. Alison and his brother Billy had only high school educations. Mr. Alison's chief sources of outside world news were the Memphis *Commercial Appeal* and the *Saturday Evening Post*. He had little time for the luxury of reading just for pleasure. He also taught a men's Bible class each Sunday at the First Methodist Church. His wife, Miss Mattilou Brown Simonton, had studied music at a Cincinnati conservatory—just as her mother, Miss Annie Lowenhaupt Brown, had. The women traveled to and from Cincinnati by Mississippi and Ohio Rivers steamboat. There was a grand piano in the Lowenhaupt parlor, and Miss Annie taught Covington and Tipton County girls for many years.

I was happy. The Leader Printing Company was, as county weeklies went, the largest and one of the best in Tennessee. I was keeping in touch with Genevieve by mail and by phone. And I was dating Mary Ann Simonton, daughter of the boss. We soon were courting. In the chill of winter, we took walks together, even in the rain. Mary Ann enjoys telling people she had chosen me about five years earlier, "when he didn't dance with me at my sorority's dance at Southwestern." She also likes to say that it was at her urging that her father decided to give me a try at becoming a newspaper reporter.

I suppose Mary Ann's parents, Miss Mattilou as she was to me, and Mr. Alison, and my mother as well, foresaw the likelihood of our falling in love. And it happened. The most significant event in the 82 years I have thus far lived occurred on Friday morning, June 7, 1946. It was my marriage to Mary Ann Simonton. We were married in her parents' home at 532 Main Street. A Methodist minister united us. My mother came up from Memphis, and Mary Anne's grandmother, Annie Lowenhaupt Brown, was there. Mr. Alison gave his daughter away. My mother lent us her 1941 Ford and we drove to some little place in the Arkansas Ozarks. Mary Ann would have enjoyed an urban scene, possibly Nashville, but that would have cost more. It was also farther away and we had to be back to work on Monday.

Mary Ann and I lived first in a back bedroom at Miss Willie's. Then we rented an upstairs one-bedroom apartment at Mrs. Bessely's on North Maple. For a refrigerator, we had a little red aluminum icebox we bought from Coca-Cola. Soon we moved to Mrs. Shelton's, a few doors north of the Simonton home. We were there until we left in the summer of 1948 for my new job on the *Chattanooga Times*. Mary Ann got pregnant right away, and carried the baby, a little boy, to full term, but he died after three days. He is buried in Covington's Munford Cemetery.

Two memorable reporting jobs stand out in memory. One was of a very drunk U.S. Congressman making a fool of himself at an all-male dinner one evening at the local hotel, the Hotel Lindo. There were those in the office and among the congressman's hearers who thought we ought not to have reported it. They believed I ought not to tattle on the old guy. I was feeling righteous, thinking that a congressman ought to behave better, so I wrote him up. Mr. Alison stood by me, and I doubt if we lost a reader.

He was what we call a Bourbon Democrat, a more conservative type. They came on not long after the Civil War. Southerners were without representation in the Congress for some years, as part of our punishment. It varied from state to state. Tennessee got back in around 1870. Some of the others were many years later being brought back into Sunday school class, so to speak.

The second memorable job—a greater and worthier one—came right after one of the first postwar local elections. Veterans everywhere were coming to the defense of democracy at home, sometimes with guns in hand, against the old-style corruption. In the Tipton County election—it was the August election—veterans in a remote precinct in the southwest corner of the county thought they saw the ballot box being stuffed, filled with votes not cast by registered voters. To prevent their being counted, so the story came to me, a war veteran called Big Boy Ballard grabbed the ballot box and fled with it to a place unknown.

I determined to try to get the story—and the ballot box. I drove alone to Big Boy's home. I had to park a long way from the house. It was in the fields out from the little town of Drummonds, and I walked uncertainly toward Big Boy's door. I didn't know Big Boy. Was he a giant? Ferocious? Hostile? Would he believe that I was not for or against him? It was over briefly, easily. I got Big Boy's side of the story and wrote it all up. I even got the ballot box.

A year or so later, much to my surprise, I heard *Memphis Press-Scimitar* editor Ed Meeman telling me, as we talked in his office, that he had read my story and ordered a follow-up in the *Press- Scimitar*. Still many more years later, when I was farming in the Tipton County community, I met other members of the large and respected Ballard family, and we got along fine.

There was freedom at the *Leader* under Mr. Alison for some imaginative writing; not taking liberties with serious news matters, of course, but in little essays for the editorial or op-ed pages. An early one, probably as good as I ever did, and I doubt that I could recover a copy of it, was a piece I wrote for the paper at Halloween time. I evoked, or tried to evoke, many of the traditional, happy Halloween images—ghosts, autumn fires, autumn leaves, the first chilly nights. The piece brought many unexpected expressions of pleasure and approval.

One afternoon after dinner at the Simonton home, Mr. Allison accompanied me back to the *Leader*. On this particular day I broached the subject of my buying an interest in the *Leader*. Mr. Alison replied that his three brothers, Joe, Billy, and Marion, each had an interest in the paper. They had gone without dividends all through the Depression years, so he didn't feel like asking any of them to sell.

Thinking about it years later, I might have assumed that Mary Ann would inherit shares, and some of the brothers might eventually want to sell. But in 1948, at the age of twenty-nine, I thought I should move on. I had done a good job at the *Leader*, won prizes from the Tennessee Press Association for my writing, and I also liked the idea of working in a bigger city. Maybe I dreamed of making it someday to New York or Washington.

I spoke with Ed Meeman, of the *Press-Scimitar*. The *Press-Scimitar* was a fine newspaper, but truth was I didn't think I was ready for Memphis. I composed a letter to send to editors of three other newspapers in Tennessee. All sent word: "Come for an interview." I had three job offers from those three interviews. The *Knoxville News Sentinel* editor, Loye Mille, offered me his top beat, at City Hall. Johnson City's *Press Chronicle* offered me a job. So did the *Chattanooga Times*. I chose the *Times*.

The fact that the paper was owned by the *New York Times* was a factor in my choosing the *Chattanooga Times*. It was a morning newspaper and had a fine reputation. They may have even offered me a little more money than the *Knoxville Sentinel*. I started at $72.50 a week. I figured the paper that offered the most money—however little more it might be—wanted me more than the others. The managing editor, Jimmy Jarvis, said, "If you come here we don't put you on the street. You have to work for a year on the desk to learn what the heck it's all about." There, well supervised, I would absorb the paper's editorial policies, and learn about the community and the lives of the often quoted personalities, public and private. His challenge appealed to me and gave me more reason to want to join the team.

Mary Ann stayed put at our Covington apartment while I boarded in Chattanooga and looked for a place for us to live. I had to choose between an apartment on McCallie Avenue or one on Cameron Hill, both in walking distance to the *Times*. We did not own a car then, borrowing my mother's 1941 Ford coach for our travels. I decided on the apartment at Cameron Hill.

In June, 1948, we drove to Chattanooga, taking a vacation along the way. We stayed in the Smokey Mountains at Gatlinburg: I fished in Cade's Cove, seeing a pool full of trout who stared back at me and would not touch the lure I threw them. We were there when the Berlin airlift began.

Reporters worked late afternoons and nights on the copy desk ("on the rim") of a morning newspaper. The editorial room of our paper, it's worth noting, was a small, badly lighted space on a mezzanine. The building also housed the afternoon paper, the *Chattanooga News-Free Press*, a cozy arrangement forced by economics.

My first assignment was to write an obituary on the wife of a prominent person. They sent me all the way to Lookout Mountain to interview a relative. I ended up burying the woman on the wrong day. I should have said, "What day of the week was this, or day of the month," but I didn't. Luckily nothing came of it.

Whenever I had to drive somewhere, I would go in the Pontiac that belonged to the *Times*. It had a siren, which I had the pleasure of using whenever I substituted for the regular police reporter, Alex Corliss. He was a sophisticated, hard-nosed guy, and taught me much about the job.

The *Times* was a small, liberal newspaper. The word *liberal* had a little shinier image then than it does now. I got my liberal leanings from my mother. She had voted for Norman Thomas on the Socialist ticket in 1932 and was active in the teacher's association. They didn't want to call it a union. It wasn't hard to think of oneself as a liberal in the days of Franklin D. Roosevelt.

I respected everybody I worked with. The general manager, in effect the publisher, was Charles McDonald Puckette. He was a handsome man, old enough to be the father of some of us. Very dignified. He was nice; he had a sense of humor. He had spent maybe twenty, thirty years up at the *New York Times*. They told him, "Hey, we need somebody running things down there in Chattanooga." He was the son of an Episcopal bishop from South Carolina, and closely connected with the University of the South. (I think his son was later made dean of the college, or vice chancellor.)

Jimmy Jarvis was a tubby, short, kind-hearted man. He had a bit of a drinking habit. Mr. Fitz, one of the older men, was the tri-state editor; he left each night to catch a Greyhound bus home. Fred Hixson, a political writer, was fat, jovial, rather well-pleased with himself in an inoffensive way. He later made an unsuccessful run for Congress. Spring Gibson, on the city hall beat, was tall, skinny, and liberal, and one of the ablest. Norman Bradley was assistant editor of the editorial page. He became editor following the retirement of Alfred Mynders, a liberal and son of S. A. Mynders, founder of the West Tennessee Normal School. Charles Bartlett, a supremely self-confident fellow, came from a rich Chicago family, graduated from Princeton, and dressed in the ultra-fashionable Ivy League collegiate style. Bartlett was a friend of John Kennedy's and left Chattanooga shortly to be a Washington correspondent; he became famous for a time. Ben Golden, on the advertising staff, was fortune hunting; he was an ex-GI who had married Ruth Sulzberger.[15]

Soon I was assigned to county government, which I loved. I had a close connection with the county judge, a guy named Wilkes Thrasher. He was a shrewd old politician. He gave me a scoop (which I don't remember), but it was a big deal for him and the *Times* too. Another one of my buddies was Ralston Schoolfield, who got himself elected as a criminal court judge. Ralston and another fellow named Charlie Coburn, a lawyer, and I were good friends. We ate lunch together and did other things. Later on I was happy to forget my association with Ralston because he ran for governor or something on the right wing segregationist ticket. He ended up as sort of a nut.

Things got tricky in those days. There was a guy—an automobile dealer, something like that—who got to be president of the county school board. I was covering county schools. I found out that he had encouraged the Ku Klux Klan to intimidate the parents of children who weren't regularly attending school. I don't know if they actually visited the homes wearing their white KKK costumes. He thought he was doing a good thing: "Get those kids in school!" We wrote a big story about it. It turned out to be a one-day story; the citizens of Chattanooga didn't care. But he did quit using the Ku Klux Klan to push his agenda.

Our apartment was part of a triplex located at 401 West Second Street. We had the top front part of the building built near the top of Cameron Hill. A nice older couple, the Brewers, lived across the hall from us. The landlord, a lawyer, and another Ku Klux Klansman, occupied the downstairs. The back of the house stood against a precipitous slope that led down to a bend on the Tennessee River where the cedar bucket factory was located; the air always had a nice scent. Just up the hill was a small public park.

We were fairly high up the hill, and our living room and bedroom faced south. The windows were large, and so were the rooms. Our living room had an east-facing window, the bedroom a west-facing one. We had an entry hall, the kitchen opening off it as well as our living room, a few feet farther on. We were free to paint the walls, and we painted our living room a deep red. We promptly entertained the whole editorial staff of the *Chattanooga Times* there on our first Christmas in Chattanooga. We packed that little two-room place with twenty-five or thirty people. Charles McDonald Puckette, a bit elderly, came with his wife to our crowded party, a very gracious act.

We didn't own a car, at least not at first. I rode a bicycle, and Mary Ann had to walk or take a taxi. It was great to ride to work at five o'clock in the afternoon and go coasting down the hill the mile or so to the newspaper. I didn't mind riding home after dark, at around two or three o'clock in the morning. I never gave it a thought, not even when it was raining. Nor was I bothered by the long, uphill pull. I was young then. After a few months of walking and biking, we bought a 1949 Ford, brand-new: a black, two-door car, a coach. We were lucky to get it, as cars were still not as plentiful as they soon became. I remember that there were more buyers than cars; I might have received some preference as a newspaperman.

It was a very happy time for me, and I think for Mary Ann. On April 26, 1950, Mary Ann gave birth to our daughter, Martha Bonner Spence. I remember her arrival at Baroness Erlanger Hospital in Chattanooga as if it were yesterday. At about 7:30 a.m., after a long and anxious night, I stood outside the delivery room as Marty was being born. A kind nurse brought her to the door to show me. What a beautiful baby!

We brought our baby girl home to 401 West Second. Memories of caring for Marty are vivid for both of us. Diapers in those days were cotton and reusable, and I rinsed many a didie; I also warmed many a bottle. I reluctantly confess that I was impatient with Marty when she didn't drink all her bottle; I thought it was important for her to get it all. We had nice friends there. Though Mary Ann had grown up as a Methodist, we decided to go to the Episcopal Church that was in walking distance. Rev. Thorne Sparkman was a fine minister. We met two nice couples. It was a sweet, easy life. We never gave any thought to money.

During our time there, I bought a lot on the west brow of Lookout Mountain, one of the last remaining there, from the Ochs or Sulzberger family, owners of the *Times*. It was a big lot with a view, and I paid only $3,000 for it. I talked to an architect. The family assumed, as we did, that we were taking root in Chattanooga. I had no idea that Mary Ann and Marty and I would ever leave Chattanooga.

But at the same time I felt pressured to return to Memphis. Thoughts of my mother living out her days alone in Memphis compelled me to think of trying to work on a Memphis paper. Years later, in a telephone conversation with Sulzberger, I got a hint that maybe they had resented my buying their lot and then leaving their newspaper. My impression was they thought I was a real comer and hoped I might someday be their editor or something. But my decision to come back to Memphis was one of conscience, not one of money.

So early in 1951, I very carefully crafted a one-page letter to Frank Ahlgren, editor of the *Commercial Appeal*, and I sent the same letter to the editor of the *Memphis Press-Scimitar*. Both editors replied they were interested in hiring me. The *Press-Scimitar* was the better of the two local papers, though it never matched the *Commercial Appeal* in circulation. The logistics were against it, being that it was an afternoon paper. The *Commercial Appeal* had the big overnight circulation in Mississippi, Arkansas, and West Tennessee, which an afternoon paper just couldn't get. But the *Press-Scimitar* was the paper that fought Ed Crump's political machine. That made it attractive to me.

I rode the Greyhound to Memphis for interviews with Ahlgren and Meeman. Ahlgren offered more money, $100 a week. But he wanted me to enroll at Memphis State and get a college degree; he was requiring that of all his new reporters. And working on a morning newspaper usually means night work. Meeman offered $93 a week. I'm not sure what assignment Meeman offered, but I took his offer. Meeman was very pleased that I came to work for the *Press-Scimitar*. In one interview he said, "You know I offered you this job in 1948." I said, "You did?" I didn't know it. Or if I knew it, I knew in my mind I wasn't ready to come back to Memphis.

I rode back to Chattanooga that night. It was a very uneasy trip. I realized I did not really want to leave Chattanooga. But Mary Ann would be only forty miles from her parents in Covington. I would be near my mother. And I would be back in the city where my father and mother had met and married and where I had attended school from the first grade almost all the way through college.

I was home.

Chapter Sixteen

Back in Memphis

I hunted for a permanent house in Memphis for Mary Ann and Marty and me, and found a house at 1565 Vinton, only two miles from the house I grew up in. Some people thought this old midtown area was deteriorating. To the unknowing, it appeared to be "that old boardinghouse neighborhood." True, in the World War II years many residents opened their large—and sometimes rundown—homes to renters, as both a patriotic and economic effort. The neighborhood could have gone the way of similar neighborhoods in other cities, and become populated primarily by renters in multifamily housing. I did not agree. I knew the area from my college days, even my days at Central High School. Vinton had been a fashionable street in a topflight neighborhood when it was born, about 1905, I believe. The first residents in the neighborhood were Memphis's "first citizens." A bank president was the first owner of our house. Many still lived here in 1952. They were country club folks: judges, lawyers, business owners, and my mother's friend and mentor, our city schools superintendent R. L. Jones. Girls I dated in my dating years lived in these houses.

And the house was big and handsome. It was a "foursquare," eight-room, two-story, stone veneer and clapboard house, sitting on a 50-by-132-foot lot that was typical for the neighborhood, though small by later standards. The houses on the street dated from the pre-automobile era, the time when streetcars carried more people than cars did. Most had driveways, but this one had a two-car garage reached by a short drive down the alley. It had a spacious front porch, close to Vinton but high above the street (these houses, like the house I grew up in, were built in the days before bulldozers, which meant the lots could not be graded easily and were usually left as is). The dining room could double as a sitting room, with a fireplace, a bay window that was three windows wide, and double sliding doors separating it from the living room.

Nonetheless, it was a bit iffy choosing this house, which meant I got a good deal. The moneylenders then did not foresee that this neighborhood would remain attractive to middle-income buyers. I paid $16,700 for the house, making a substantial down payment of about one-half the price of the house. Mary Ann insists to this day that she was totally surprised to learn that I had bought a house, not to mention one in which she was an overnight guest during her years as a student at Southwestern College, 1939 to 1942. As it turned out, I was right: Vinton and the surrounding streets, later called the Central Gardens District, reverted to a stable, mostly single-family area.

We were living at the time in an apartment on South Parkway. Mary Ann was pregnant with our second child. On a Saturday morning in January 1952 we moved, with help from Mary Ann's brother, Alison Simonton. John W. Spence Jr., whom we call John Jr., was born at Baptist Hospital on March 28, 1952. He was Mary Ann's third pregnancy, and third caesarian. She was brave to have a third child after having had two surgical deliveries already, and having lost one baby. The birth went according to schedule. His homecoming to 1565 Vinton put a seal on our new purchase.

My new boss, Ed Meeman, was a physically small man. He never married, but lived with his mother, sister, and brother. Meeman came from the *Knoxville News Sentinel*, which he had founded. Before that he had been at Evansville, Illinois. He was a protégé of Edward Scripps, and a most deserving one. Edward Scripps was a much finer newspaperman than his chosen successor, Roy Howard. Mr. Meeman thought highly of Scripps, and Scripps thought highly of him. In 1921 or 1922, Scripps sent Meeman to Knoxville with a package of money and nothing else and told him to start a newspaper, which he did. It was Knoxville's only evening paper then. In 1931, he came to Memphis; Scripps realized Memphis was a bigger place than Knoxville and probably thought that Meeman could make the *Press-Scimitar* surpass the *Commercial Appeal*. But he never did. Aside from the logistics, there was the politics. Most Memphians probably approved of the influence-wielding political boss Ed Crump and therefore of the newspaper that supported him, the *Commercial Appeal*.

The *Commercial Appeal* won an undeserved reputation for liberality back in the 1920s when it fought the Ku Klux Klan. It won a Pulitzer Prize for that. But it fought the Klan because the paper's editor, P. J. Mooney, was a Catholic. The Klan was after Mooney, so Mooney went after the Klan. I don't think that's the official history, but that's my recollection.

Meeman was proud of how he got Shelby Forest to become a state park. That was a major thing with him. I heard him tell the story many times. He was at his desk one late afternoon. (This was in 1938.) A man came in and said, "I'm representing the Park Service, and I've been looking all over for a site for a state forest. I haven't found one." Meeman said, "I've got just the place for you." So Meeman showed him Shelby Forest and the man said, "This is it." That was the birth of what today is named the Meeman-Shelby Forest State Park, one of Memphis's finest treasures.

Meeman had his home out there, or had determined to have his home out there. His first home here in town stood near the corner of Summer and Graham Streets. It was a spacious place. Meeman always loved the suburbs. When he went to Shelby Forest, it was country. There was a joke that Ed Crump would not pave North Main Street or North Second Street because he wanted Mr. Meeman to have a bumpy ride into town.

Over the years I became very close to Ed Meeman. I had won his respect early on, differing with him and having the courage to say so. Most others on the editorial staff were yes men, and Meeman knew it. Meeman was very kind to me, coping with my late arrivals at work by keeping me late in the afternoon. We then discussed and wrote editorials. One of Meeman's sayings was, "A man convinced against his will is of the same opinion still." Whenever I disagreed with him he would write the editorial himself. He liked short editorials as a rule, holding them to three hundred or so words. On the rare occasion he felt required it, an editorial could run a whole column, even more than a column.

The publishing company building housed the editorial staffs of the newspaper and the advertising department, as well as the presses. It was an old auto assembly plant located on the south side of Union Avenue, on a railroad spur that brought the giant paper rolls to the presses. A memory I enjoy is that of seeing the county political boss E. W. Hale stop on Union Avenue each afternoon, get out of his car, deposit his coins into a newspaper box and get his *Press-Scimitar.* I liked Hale, a man who left the talking to others. He was, of course, overshadowed by Crump, but Hale knew his strengths.

The newspaper then had several other recently hired fellows. They were Milton Britten, Tom Huser, Charlie Caldwell—all congenial men. Veteran reporters included the inimitable Clark Porteous, along with Tom Meanley, Paul Fairleigh, Ed Topp, and others. Soon I was awarded a choice desk across from Tom Meanley, which put me close to the city desk and also close to Meeman's "ice box," as we called it, because it was at the time the only air-conditioned office in the building. Later, the whole fifth floor was cooled, a costly job because the printers and linotypes were just below, producing a lot of heat.

The paper didn't give me any special assignment. Early on I was treated by the city editor and the managing editor like a cub reporter, which I certainly was not. I had a lot of time to do what I thought would be fun or productive, and I had to take a little time to be assigned here and there and yonder.

The city editor was Null Adams, who had not gone beyond high school. His younger brother was city editor of the *Commercial Appeal*. They came from South Memphis, and were tough, working-class people. A lot of newspapermen in the early days had limited educations, but they had keen minds and courage and a real interest in things.

I took my orders day by day from Adams. But as city editor, he would have gotten his orders from the managing editor and Mr. Meeman. There was a daily editorial conference. Occasionally I was in on them. When Mr. Meeman wanted a discussion over an issue, in order to make his decision he'd have us in, five or six of us. He'd say, "Now I want to hear what you think, but I'm going to make the decision." We might have five people saying, "This is what you ought to do." He was a real open-minded, fair sort of a person. He could hear people's arguments. But he was boss. That was his job. And if he didn't want to do it, he didn't. I'm sure Frank Ahlgren at the *Commercial Appeal* would say the same thing. It was not a democracy. There isn't much that's democratic in this world.

One day the city editor assigned me and a young woman who was a photographer, Lil (Lillian) Foscue, to do a series on the county schools. It seems Adams did not tell Meeman he was doing that, or Meeman forgot it. Null Adams was a very liberal person. Why he favored my producing that series, I don't really know. Lil and I produced a five-day series of stories making clear how inferior some of the schools were. This was 1952, and the racial segregation issue had not taken hold of popular imagination. The series documented the poor facilities without focusing on race.

We started working on it in the spring while school was in session. The weather must have been moderate. I don't remember getting caught in sleet or snow, or in downpours, or looking at any potbelly stoves. That's what they had in the black schools. They were shabby compared to the white schools. They had outdoor toilets. Some of them had only one electric light hanging from the ceiling. They were just leftover things. The white schools were far better. The county school superintendents, for many years, were women—my mother's friends and my friends. I don't recall any conversations about the conditions of the black schools. Race was a subject that was more felt than discussed. We just had persisted so long in seeing ourselves as different sorts of human beings.

I never felt any resistance from the black community when I was investigating the black schools. The teachers and principals were delighted at any prospect of somebody paying any attention to them and bettering their condition. I didn't see it as a racial issue so much. It was fair play. Essentially it was an inventory task. No one could argue with the high number of outdoor toilets and cold-water kitchens in the schools.

Meeman was surprised to see the series, and he had reservations about running it. He called me into the icebox to discuss whether to run the stories or not. It was late afternoon. Conferences between Meeman and me seemed always to come then, when most of the staff were gone and the final edition was off the press. We sat across from each other, as we did during many one-to-one sessions that he and I would have over the next ten years. I reminded him of why I had chosen his newspaper. This was impudent and unfair of me. "I came to work on the *Press-Scimitar* because of my respect for your courage," I told him. He knew it was true, that Ahlgren had offered me a top reporting assignment. Mr. Meeman, of course, had a far clearer idea than I of the Memphis and Mid-South social outlook. He may have wondered about cancellations of subscriptions or boycotts, or at least letters and calls from segregationist subscribers.

I was playing my ace card, and he went for it. He ran the series on page one, for five days. He placed my picture and a brief description of me next to the stories: that I was a white Southerner writing about the black schools, that I was a war veteran, and by implication a patriot. He did not want readers thinking I was some outside agitator, as was popular then to call anyone who rocked the boat in any way.

From the Memphis Press-Scimitar, March 3, 1952

A Story of Outdoor Toilets, Pumps, Coal Stoves and Overcrowding
By John Spence

Outdoor toilets, old-fashioned pumps in the yard, coal stoves in the classroom. Two teachers to a room. Two children to a seat.

These are some of the things you see on a visit to three county schools for negro children. These three are Brooks Avenue, Weaver and White's Chapel.

"Look at Geeter, Barret's Chapel, Woodstock and Millington while you're at it," County School Supt. George Barnes asked.

Four Have What All Should
We did. These four, with a few minor deficiencies, are as fine as the county's better schools for white children. They have indoor toilets, running water, kitchens that are bright and clean to fix hot lunches. They have gymnasiums, three of them built in less than two years.

In fact, they have all the things that the other 40 negro schools should have. And then some.

But these four were the only up-to-standard schools among 25

visited before these reports were written. Seeing them only heightens the contrast with the others.

Barnes has begun a program of improvement. He intends to continue it, he says. But he cannot do it out of current revenue. Shelby County Court has not yet called for a bond referendum. The court's next regular meeting is in April.

Lacking in Almost All Facilities
These are the facts:

Twenty-one negro schools visited lack almost every facility for comfort, health, and efficiency.

They have:

No hot lunches.

No hand-washing or water-heating facilities.

No central heating, not even state-recommended air-circulating jackets on the coal stoves which are the rule.

No indoor toilets.

No adequate lighting.

Eight are entirely without lights though electric lines pass in front of some, near others. A store not 20 yards from the unlighted Mt. Pisgah School has had lights for 18 years.

Most Are Overcrowded

Most schools are overcrowded. One, Brunswick, has five classrooms, 394 pupils. The auditorium here, as in most schools that have an auditorium, is used for classes. Two teachers and their classes use it at the same time, all the time.

Many schools' electric lights have been installed by teachers, parents and pupils.

One hand-operated pump provides drinking water for 394 children at one school.

Only two of these schools—out in the country—have grounds comparable in size with those City of Memphis has gotten for its new schools.

Policy is not the same for all schools. The county installs lights, provides shades at some. It lets others provide their own, goes 50-50 sometimes.

Schools that formerly served hot lunches are legally barred from doing so now. They have fallen behind advancing state standards.

A church has served as school at Frayser for seven years.

Not an A-1 Negro High School

Not a negro high school in Shelby County outside the city has an A-1 rating from the state. All white high schools do. Not one negro high school (there are only three, with a fourth coming in next fall) is recognized by the Southern Association of Colleges and Secondary Schools. All white high schools are.

Children in the Collierville area must travel over 20 miles to Geeter High.

Books outmoded in white schools are used in negro schools. Even with old books, there are not enough.

Teachers have 57, 72, 58, 44 in a class.

At Capleville, a few pupils walk six miles to school. State law requires either transportation or a school nearer the child.

Collierville School, 31 years old, has interior walls that have never been painted. A garage is used for a classroom.

Walls Unpainted 22 Years

At McKinney School, walls have gone unpainted for 22 years. Shelby-Bailey School has never been painted inside in nearly 30 years.

Outdoor toilets serve 529 children at Weaver School.

There is no choice of subjects for ninth and 10th graders at several schools. Agriculture and home economics are the only vocational subjects.

At Germantown, two teachers teach five grades in one room at one time. A pipeline has brought running water to the yard for about 20 years. Still there are no inside drinking fountains, wash basins, toilets or kitchen sinks.

Best negro schools are found in communities where, the teachers said, white citizens took an interest.

Going back to where this reporter started, at Brooks Avenue, Weaver and White's Chapel schools, let's have a look:

You see fresh paint, ample light thru windows, electric lights for rainy days, and good order maintained in the classes.

Coal Stoves, Room Full of Smoke

But at Brooks, a three teacher, eight-grade school in sight of Memphis, coal stoves heat the building. One room was foggy with smoke. A teacher said the flue was bad.

Gas heat which could replace the coal is not more than 150 yards from the school.

There is no all-weather walk to the outdoor privies. The land the school is on is low, but there is more than enough land for a septic tank field (for indoor toilets) as large as those serving some eating places and night clubs which have more customers than Brooks has students.

The frame building is in good

repair. It stands on piers, however. This makes heating more costly and increases the fire hazard; also the insurance rate.

Tho there are electric lights in the building, there is no electric pump on the well. Children pump it by hand. No drinking fountain was visible.

The school has no facilities for serving hot lunches.

About 95 children attend.

Addition Just Completed

At White's Chapel, on Sewanee Road south of Fields Road, there is a four-classroom addition just completed last spring. At Weaver, on Weaver south of Mitchell, there are gas space heaters installed last spring.

Weaver had 529 net enrollment at last report. Thirteen teachers hold classes in eight rooms and auditorium.

It is also a frame building, on piers. The paint job looks fresh and good. Students do the clean-up work at Weaver. One teacher said it is a good thing: Children can be taught cleanliness by doing.

Two pumps, hand-operated, supply the drinking water for the more than 500 children. From a concrete trough the children get their water as some teacher or older child pumps.

The active PTA gave the

school a stove and refrigerator. But lack of running water and sanitary disposal makes it illegal to serve regular hot lunches.

529 Children—Outdoor Toilets
This school for 529 children uses outdoor toilets.

White's Chapel has about 215 on roll. It has electric lights, but is also without an electric pump on the well. It has no cafeteria, no indoor toilets. Coal stoves heat it.

White's Chapel closed for cotton picking last fall. The school serves Boxtown community. Most parents work in the city, not on farms, the principal said.

Fairness is a strong impulse in the American people. They know whenever somebody's getting the short end of it, and they usually react. People say, "Hey, let's shape up." The stories I wrote weren't intended to create integration. Our interest was fairness. This was in 1952. We didn't get the Supreme Court decision until 1954. All I was interested in was getting these children a fair shake, to see to it that those kids got just as good books, just as good lighting and plumbing as the white schools. I didn't challenge separate but equal. Our stories didn't deal with the overall issue. They simply focused on the abysmal conditions in these schools. In the city and county, people responded. They said, "We ought to give them better schools." And they did.

The series established my reputation with many readers, in a favorable way. But one reader, whose views were reported in a weekly column, suggested the paper might also want to report the fact that outdoor toilets were not unusual and could be found in the homes of the white citizenry. True, but they were not to be found in the segregated white public schools. We also received numerous anonymous hate calls on our home telephone from people who called us "nigger" lovers, or commies, or told us to leave town. May Ann would thank them for calling and hang up. She told our son that if we acted as if we weren't afraid or unhappy about the getting the calls, the hate callers would get frustrated and stop bothering us.

The series gained circulation for the paper in the large black community. For years afterward blacks considered me their best friend in the newspaper business. I was asked to join the board of the Memphis Urban League. I was, if I remember right, the second white person on the board. The first was a tall, courageous old man, Edwin Dalstrom, of Scandinavian ancestry. His speech was different from that of Southerners. He was one of the seven men and one woman (Frances Coe) who defied the Ed Crump regime in Memphis. Dalstrom's company was based in another city, so it was immune to the power of Crump's regime. The black members of the Urban League board were, in my eyes, courageous men: Taylor Hays, J. A. McDaniel, Hollis F. Price are the ones I remember.

The series on the Shelby County schools also made my reputation as a newspaperman and a Memphis citizen. The articles also got me invited to join the Memphis Committee on Community Relations, a group of white and black leaders formed to help desegregate the schools. Soon afterward I was given the City Hall desk and there I was allowed to do pretty much whatever I wanted.

Though it was my concern for Mother that had brought me back to Memphis, ironically I did not see as much of her as I might have. She was aging. She lived in our house at 1422 Faxon Avenue and kept driving as long as she could. My cousins were very kind to her. That was a wonderful blessing for her and them. They admired her, enjoyed her. She kept people laughing and enjoying life.

Her last days were spent in a nursing home. In 1963 she moved out of her home and lived in our house on Vinton for a short time, here in this room where I work. Mary Ann felt the burden. Our good doctor Henry Gotten said, "It's either you or her. Put her in the nursing home." Mother stayed first in one nursing home and then in another. I didn't like the first place; I wasn't crazy about the second one either. She died on August 30, 1963.

Chapter Seventeen

Covering Politics

So far at the *Press-Scimitar*, I had managed to operate pretty much in smooth waters. After all, I was the new kid on the block and allowed to choose my topics. People were mostly encouraging. The series on the county schools got their attention, but that was all objective reporting. All that changed when I was assigned to City Hall. That's when I started getting resistance. "There's that guy from the *Press-Scimitar*," they would say. Any reporter from the *Press-Scimitar* was *persona non grata* with city and county officials. City Hall was Mr. Crump's territory; the county folks were Mr. Crump's people. They favored the mealy mouthed *Commercial Appeal*, which was kind to Mr. Crump.

Everything had come through Mr. Crump in Memphis from about 1927 to 1954. Edward Hull Crump was from Holly Springs, Mississippi. If he had a church affiliation I never found out what it was. How he got away with this, I don't know. His excuse for not going to church on Sunday was that he had to drive from Memphis to Holly Springs every Sunday to visit his mama. He was ousted from the office of mayor in 1915, because he didn't enforce the prohibition law. That's not popularly discussed in Memphis. It didn't faze Ed Crump a bit. He just turned around and became county trustee and made thousands of dollars as county trustee. About 1928 he went into the insurance business with the Trezvants, who are still in real estate and insurance. Whether he foresaw that all the underlings and everybody who wanted a city job would buy their insurance from him, I don't know. But that happened. It became sort of an insurance policy to buy your insurance from Ed Crump. He made a fortune in the insurance business.

Beginning in 1935 when he left Congress after serving two terms, Crump held no public title. He called the shots by phone and in person, from his fifth floor office at the northeast corner of Main and Adams. He could deliver sixty thousand votes and the other guy would get none. He kept that office as long as he lived. People would bow their heads in that direction. His name was like God. You didn't use it carelessly. "The man on the corner," was one of the ways they spoke of him. The man on the corner. They'd lower their voice and tilt their heads at a certain angle. He was so powerful that people didn't really want to use his name. Sometimes they'd say "Mr. Crump," in a low voice. They'd also just nod their head. You were supposed to know who they meant, where they were pointing. It was amusing to me that so many people were reluctant to use his name. But he was ever-present in the minds of those who dealt with the city. I don't know who named him Boss Crump.

My only contact with Crump came when my mother and I visited him in 1934 to ask for an appointment at the U.S. Military Academy at West Point. Now, as a city hall reporter, I never dealt with him face to face. I certainly wasn't reluctant to meet him. He made only one direct approach to me. I think he was fussing at me. I fussed back and that was it. I didn't hear from him again.

Crump had at least two sons. His younger son, an amateur flyer, was killed in a plane crash. This was about 1939. The myth is that the tragedy instilled Mr. Crump with religion, from which he got the idea to run all the whores out of town. He had an older son named Edward Hull Crump Jr., who succeeded Crump in the insurance business and lived into the 1980s.

Crump left a mixed legacy. A dictatorship runs against the grain of democracy. I think that hurt Memphis and the state of Tennessee. Many, such as my wife Mary Ann, thought Mr. Crump was satisfactory because he employed people who were reformed alcoholics and they worked hard.

The *Press-Scimitar* had two, three, sometimes four city hall reporters. My colleagues were Charles Caldwell, Milton Briton, and for a time, Tom Huser. We had another fellow with us for a while. We all worked very amiably, covering courts as well as the administrative offices. We sometimes lunched together at the Claridge Hotel, just a block away from Main and Adams.

Both the city and county governments were housed in the same building. I dealt with the mayor, the city commissioners, and the city treasurer, also the county folks, such as the county court clerk. If they were in that building, they were fair game. I wouldn't go to see anyone else, say the chancellery court clerk, if he wasn't on my beat. If I had an issue I'd first check it out with the guys I shared the beat with. The pressroom for the *Press-Scimitar* was a coat closet off of a jury room on the third floor of City Hall. The *Commercial Appeal* had considerably better quarters. I eventually became friends with those guys.

The mayor in 1951 and 1952 was Watkins Overton, a small man from a founding Memphis family. He worked under Crump's thumb. His comptroller was Frank Tobey, an able, honest man, a big, heavy-set person. As comptroller, Tobey managed and disbursed city funds. He saw to it that there was no graft, no stealing. He was the most honest of Crump's people in city government. The most helpful persons in city government worked in the comptroller's office. Tobey's staff was small: about four aides, two of whom were women, very competent. Tobey always trusted and respected the reporters. He went to great lengths to see that we understood what we were writing about. He invited us to his small home some evenings to explain to us and educate us. Whether we of the *Press-Scimitar* were favored, I'm not sure. I think we were. I don't remember how Mayor Overton left office, but it was abruptly. Crump appointed Tobey to his place. Sad to say, Tobey died of a heart attack soon after becoming mayor.

I did have difficulties. There was a woman who worked for the county trustee. I don't recall what the issue was, but there was something smelly. I went to see her. She knew I was coming and ducked out of her office, leaving papers on the table. I went ahead and looked, which was probably unethical; I shouldn't have done it. They apparently had some way of observing that room and I was caught. That infuriated her boss. He wanted to have a knockdown, drag out fight with me. He was bigger than I was, too. I didn't relish that prospect, so I didn't allow him his chance.

On October 16, 1954, at about 4:00 p.m., Edward Hull Crump died. He was eighty. Because Crump lived on Peabody Avenue near my home, Mr. Meeman felt free to ask me to patrol the Crump residence so as to be the first with the news of Crump's death. Charles Caldwell, a very able newspaperman, was on duty that afternoon, and he got us a fine "extra," the last one the *Press-Scimitar* ever printed.

In 1955, reform forces seized the opportunity and put Edmund Orgill in the mayor's office. He had been the president of the Chamber of Commerce and the head of one of the biggest businesses in town. He changed from all that to becoming a leader for civil rights and the Democratic Party. He became a true believer in civil rights, and much more liberal. In time Orgill became a warm personal friend. His wife, Catherine, called him Edmund, and so I did as she did. I was often in their home at 1490 Linden, a few blocks from ours. Orgill called me Johnny. Nobody else did, not even Catherine.

Ed Orgill had a good sense of humor. He had a gravelly voice; he was not a good public speaker. But there was a real bond of respect and affection there. His tenure as mayor was hindered by lack of support from four city commissioners. These were John "Buddy" Dwyer, Claude Armour, Stanley Dillard, and Henry Loeb. They overturned progressive moves Orgill made, thus marring his administration. Orgill's term ended in 1959 and he did not seek reelection.

In 1960, Ed ran for governor. His friend Estes Kefauver, one of Tennessee's U.S. senators, asked Edmund to do that, wanting a friend in the governor's office when he, Estes, ran again in 1960. I covered Edmund's race, often riding with him and Catherine in Ford cars lent to the campaign by Wink Bond, the Ford dealer at Arlington and friend of Estes. I recall many a time riding in the middle of the front seat with six in the car, traveling all over the state.

During the race, a Nashville politician, Clifford Allen, offered to withdraw if Edmund would promise him a post in Tennessee government. I was not in that discussion, and learned only later about it. Edmund turned Allen down. Allen stayed in, drawing away a sufficient number of votes to barely defeat Orgill and elect Beauford Ellington to the governor's office.

Around that time Kefauver, through his able administrative assistant Richard Wallace, a former *Press-Scimitar* reporter, asked me to join Estes' senate staff. I had to say no. I could not leave Mary Ann and our two young children in Memphis, couldn't move them to Washington. My mother was still alive and alone at 1422 Faxon, and Mary Ann's folk were in Covington.

I possessed a keen nose for tomfoolery, and I found some in the county government. A quarterly county court of about nine elected persons (all men in my time) was functioning under the Tennessee Constitution as the county's governing body. In Shelby County its members simply executed the policies dictated by Crump and Hale. There was nepotism: Hale's son, E. W. Hale Jr., a lawyer, was the county attorney. Hale's two fellow commissioners were Dan Mitchell and Rudolph Jones. Jones was a lifelong county resident and landowner and engineer. Dan Mitchell, a burly, outgoing man, was an able public servant who probably owed his first county job to his aunt. Mr. Hale was an old man, way on in years, austere and dignified. Somehow he'd acquired great prestige. He was the boss man. He decided to quit. Before he left, he asked the other two, Dan and Rudolph, "Who'd you like to see take my place?"

Dan recommended his buddy Dave Harsh. Dave was a successful lawyer, pleading cases, mostly real estate. He'd been a commander in the American Legion, a World War I veteran. I had gone out with his daughter as a teenager. It had been a hot and heavy romance. Ten or fifteen years later, here he was a big shot on the county commission and I was an adversarial reporter. He took great offense at my writing. He was power hungry, and thought he'd create himself a segregationist political organization. "Keep Memphis Down in Dixie," was his slogan in one election.

When Dave came in as chairman, he wanted to have a little coffee klatch in his private office. I insisted on sitting in on it. The commissioners were permitting their little darling, the *Commercial Appeal* guy, in the meeting, so they had to let me in too. You talk about the whore in church—that was real icy. They didn't want me in there, and they radiated it. I'd go walking in there just to make a point.

I don't know if there were issues of great moment. One was secrecy—not having open meetings. There was also a question of where the money was going, and whether Harsh was trying to run roughshod over other people.

My gift for this kind of reporting got me sent on to a bigger arena. In 1953, I began covering the Tennessee legislature. Even though the paper had a small circulation, we had to cover the legislature. The legislature met every other year for a few weeks. I covered it for twelve years, from 1953 to 1965, going to Nashville during the short time it was in session, and living at the Hermitage Hotel, which stood within sight of the capitol building. I took the train up on Mondays and returned home on Fridays.

In one session there was a guy named Tom Mitchell. I wrote an unflattering story about him. Late one evening I joined some people in a restaurant. It wasn't a private gathering. Tom Mitchell came in, carrying the paper with him. He walked over to me and made like he was wiping his ass with the paper. He said, "This is what I think of the way you write." He did this in a semipublic room, in the evening. That kind of display hurt his reputation far more than it did mine.

My very first legislative assignment from Meeman was a near fateful one: I was to ask the young governor-elect, Frank Goad Clement, about the campaign contributions he had accepted from the trucking industry. Clement wanted to reward his political allies with the state's insurance contract. I had an informant. This was W. Percy MacDonald, a lobbyist for the insurance companies. Percy had talent. All the insurance companies in the state of Tennessee employed him as their lobbyist, as did all the airline companies. Insurance and aviation were his two territories. The reason he represented the airlines is he was a pioneer in aviation, both as a flyer and in getting the Memphis Municipal airport built. Percy was quite a guy. A bon vivant, he did a lot of traveling and made a good living. He was in with Crump and Hale, and was chairman of the county school board. And he took care of legislators as a lobbyist; that was his private gold mine. It was Percy who fed me the information about the insurance companies and one particular legislator that Clement was trying to favor.

One afternoon I went from state office to state office. I visited the governor's office first, and then kept going. I knew the telephone calls were going ahead of me. "Don't talk to that guy from the *Press-Scimitar*," is what they were saying. Clement was not an attractive guy. He was a glad-handing, loud kind of guy. He would routinely have his press conferences with fifteen or twenty reporters. One morning soon thereafter, he was trotting around the room shaking hands with the reporters. I was feeling irritated with him, his having done what he could to prevent my getting that story. When he got to me, I wouldn't shake hands with him. That teed him off. That was pretty near the end of that meeting. He wheeled around and said something, I don't know exactly what. A little later he was calling up Ed Meeman, saying, "I don't want this guy up here. Call him home." I waited, or rather, I went about my job, knowing I would be hearing more about this. Soon I was called to a phone, and Mr. Meeman talked to me. He told me I had done wrong, that Clement had asked him to replace me. But he had told the governor he would not. "You should have shook hands with the guy," he told me. But he stuck by me.

Clement gave the job of Controller of the Treasury to Jean Bonfitch, who campaigned ably for him. It was an important job. He put another woman in the cabinet too. And then Jean fell in love with me. I didn't realize exactly what was happening. She would come to my hotel room. I never slept with her, but I might have. She wanted to be slept with. She was a recent widow, her husband had just died. She was a real nice person. I hope she's still alive. She'd be in her eighties if she were. Our friendship was a considerable annoyance to Clement. But Jean didn't do anything disloyal. Later on she told me that he had lost his sense, in a way. He made one particularly ugly sexual exhibition of himself to her. That was the end of their friendship. Clement had courage sometimes, but he was undone by his vices. He chased skirts and he was a secret alcoholic. In 1969 Clement died in an automobile accident, probably under the influence. It happened on a rainy afternoon in Nashville. I was there at the time working on my master's degree.

He and Buford Ellington gave us what we call "leapfrog government." At the time Clement was first elected, the state constitution limited the number of terms a governor could serve. He served his limit, and then he picked his buddy Buford Ellington, who'd been his campaign manager. Buford succeeded Clement. When Buford had run his time out, Clement succeeded Buford. And then one more time, Buford succeeded Clement. They held the governor's office between them for eighteen years, from 1952 to 1970.

Buford Ellington died the right way. He had a heart attack while he was playing golf. I don't think he was in government at the time.

Chapter Eighteen

Saving the Rivers

My writing for Ed Meeman about the preservation of the Eleven Point and the Current Rivers is a high point in my journalistic career. We saved the rivers—from the popular impulse to dam every wild stream to produce electricity and recreation areas. We met great folk in the region: B. B. Morgan, and Freeman and Everlea England, a pharmacist and his wife in Pocahontas, Arkansas. I lose count now of all the lovely trips to the rivers with wonderful friends—to the Jacks Fork, the Current, the Arkansas Buffalo, the Tennessee Buffalo, the Little Swan Creek. I introduced quite a few younger men and a few of their wives to the free-flowing rivers.

Lucius Burch and George Grider Sr. had introduced me to the rivers first. Lucius Burch was a high-profile Memphis attorney and civil rights activist. He married Elsie Caldwell. She was a horsewoman, a tall brunette. She also wrote novels. As a young woman she was probably beautiful, though she became an alcoholic. They had four daughters. She and Lucius lived in a handsome old house—quite a nice sort of place out near Collierville. Lucius flew his airplane to work. For many years he flew back and forth between Collierville and Memphis, landing his plane on Mud Island. He had a boat over there. He'd land his plane, cross the Wolf River in his boat, and come trotting up to his office at the corner of Court Square and Second Street.

My earliest memories of Lucius date back to 1953 when we rode the night train to Nashville. This marked my first assignment to cover the

Tennessee Legislature. Lucius and I were fellow passengers one night. He generously shared his whisky with me before we turned in for the night.

Lucius had a great deal of courage, a great deal of intelligence, and a fine background. He had a lot of girlfriends. He wouldn't run for public office, and Meeman thought it was a shame he didn't. He told Lucius, "You would be such a fine—" and name any one of a half dozen government positions. Lucius's liberalism was mostly Libertarian rather than economic. He served as director of the National Bank of Commerce until his death. His law firm represented Standard Oil and Illinois Central Railroad. He would take a criminal defense case every now and then. Not just for anybody. It probably cost a few hundred thousand dollars to have Lucius as your criminal defense lawyer.

George Grider Sr. had been a submarine captain during the war and had recently returned to his native city of Memphis to practice law; he was working in Burch's firm. I met George in 1951 at a Great Books class at Southwestern that the Ford Foundation was financing in those days. There we discovered a mutual interest in politics. Others in the class included Frances Coe, Tom Turley, and Mary Ann Spence—all kinds of folks took part. My friendship with George was cemented at the time of the 1952 election. I remember we went to his home, 417 Prescott, to commiserate with each other because all the good guys were losing the election.

George and I flew to Missouri with Lucius Burch in his airplane one Saturday morning. I flew at the controls a bit, though not to Lucius's satisfaction. He was a bit hung over that morning. We landed on Lucius's ranch, called the Pigman. It covered nine or ten thousand acres, with considerable frontage on the Eleven Point River. It was pretty scrubby land. (Lucius had hoped to make a short-term killing feeding some cattle and seeing the price go up. It went the other way and he lost on it.) Later that day we canoed on the

Eleven Point River. It was my first time on the Eleven Point. I quite predictably capsized us. I was forgiven.

Some of the happiest memories I have are of canoe trips with George, sleeping out under the stars, getting wet in the rain. The first outing George and I undertook by ourselves was a duck hunt, in the fall of 1955. I don't know why George didn't abandon me then, because I came to the trip improperly dressed and ill equipped. George nearly killed himself trying to move the canoe through knee-deep mud with me sitting high and dry, at his insistence. We paddled in the pre-dawn darkness, down the Devil's Elbow, one of the myriad small tributaries of the Mississippi. It lies on the Arkansas side of the river and flows into the Tennessee chute. We went east across the chute and through a woods into still another chute where a few duck blinds had been built. Others had built the blinds, and George and I just borrowed them. We took George's son, George, Jr., with us on more than one occasion. He was quite young, maybe fourteen or fifteen, and it must have been quite a trial of his patience to stay with us. Not that he had any alternative once we had entered the boat. At one such outing we stopped at a general store to pick up supplies. Young George put a nickel in the jukebox and insisted we listen to a song performed by a man he called his then favorite singer. George, Sr. and I listened politely. It was the first time I'd ever heard the name Elvis Presley.

The casual gift to me from Lucius Burch of his somewhat battered 18-foot Old Town canoe was one of the most important gifts I ever received. I became known as an authority (though I was not) on float streams of our region, and I led many folk into canoeing and camping. Mary Ann, of course, was my camping partner, though not my canoeing partner; she never took to canoeing.

From the *Memphis Press-Scimitar,* April 28, 1962
Where the Indians and Buffalo Roamed
Hundred of Artifacts Are Found by MSU Archeology Students
By John Spence, Press-Scimitar Writer

Indians lived in almost every bend of one of the most beautiful river valleys within 150 miles of Memphis.

That's what Memphis State University archeology students decided from evidence found in their four-day canoe trip down the Buffalo. They brought the proof back with them, in 5-gallon lard cans and labeled paper sacks.

They found hundreds—perhaps more than 1000—spear points, hide scrapers and other lint tools, they believe were used 2000 to 7000 years ago in the woods and buffalo pastures along the swift, clear river. The Buffalo rises in Lawrence County. It meanders west thru Lewis and Wayne, then north thru Perry and Humphreys counties to join the Duck just before the Duck enters the Tennessee 10 miles south of Waverly.

Students Gerald Smith and Sims McKnight learned also that canoes do go under water when turned sideways to the current and tilted into it.

Smith's lesson was more complete than McKnight's. In fact, he just about took the whole course in canoe dunking. He and the canoe went under a huge sycamore that

had fallen into the Buffalo from the right bank below Mile 97 in Davis Bend.

Some Items Lost
There are four plastic cups, camp stove, a pair of field glasses, a compass, a pair of shoes, a snake bite kit, and quite a few other items on the bottom in that bend, if anybody wants to go after them. At that, more gear was salvaged than was lost.

The surveyors found 22 places which produced evidence that Indians lived there. Archeologists call these Indians "archaic," and say they lived before the "woodland" and the "Mississippian" Indians.

Archeologist Charles Nash of the MSU faculty organized the trip. Nash is the man who has brought Chucalissa Indian Village almost literally back to life.

Dan Printup planted the seed of the idea. Printup, photographer and amateur archeologist, found "projectile points" on the Buffalo last year. He was then on a trip with Tennessee Game and Fish Commission biologists Gene Ruhr and Mike Stubbs and Dave Murrian, photographer for the Game and Fish Commission.

Archaic Indians, by the way, did not have bows and arrows. They had spears, hence "projectile points" and not "arrow heads."

Printup and Nash thought that canoes would get more men more places faster, in the steep, winding valley of the Buffalo than cars or shoe leather would.

Not that there is any lack of passable roads; probably every one of the wide and beautiful bends in the Buffalo can be reached in a late model, low-slung car. But there would be so much back-tracking.

The 22 separate places—separated by the width of the river, or by a ridge or by miles of distance—that were proved to be Indian living places are probably less than half of the living places in the 40 miles of river covered by the expedition.

The purpose of the trip from MSU's point of view was to find the sites, collect and label artifacts on each site for laboratory examination, and do such accurate mapping of each site that others can go back to them for more thoro study.

But the trip offered so much more besides: Possibly no other stream in this region is the home of so many wood ducks. And they were having a good spring: Almost every pair had a hatch of tiny ducklings.

Beaver sign was found, and muskrat, and mink.

Smith was the best qualified ornithologist along. He identified perhaps 40 kinds of birds even tho he was concentrating on canoe handling while he was on the water and on discovering Indian artifacts while he was ashore.

By moonlight one night, while Printup turned in to sleep, the other four members of the party made their way to a landlocked little pool in the woods. The pool was left by flood stage on the Buffalo.

Speared Fish

In that pool, the men speared the fish trapped there by the falling water. And two very large snapping turtles were discovered. These, too, had to be captured for eating purposes.

Rodney Gates had discovered the fish in the pool. Now he got the turtle-cleaning job, because he was the bus driver on the trip, and—theoretically—had time to spare during the day. Gates works for the State Parks Division under Nash.

Swift-flowing streams are one-way streets. You don't paddle up them. So, at end of day, you "take out." And if you have not carried all your sleeping and cooking gear, so as to make camp, someone must meet you and take you to camp. Gates had that job of meeting us at the end of each day this trip. Next trip, one hopes, he will be aboard a canoe.

Those rivers are so beautiful, so quiet, so intriguing. I remember with joy the searches in the riverside meadows for Indian artifacts, the swims, the adventures, if you can call such little episodes *adventures*. Two in particular I remember on the Tennessee Buffalo. I led a group of six or eight of us on that trip. I don't remember the put-in, but it wasn't far above Slink Flatwoods. We picked a good campsite, unloaded all our stuff. All set. Then an overalls-wearing, taciturn man came out of the shadows. "Cain't stay here!" he told us. Darkness descending. Load up. Paddle furiously on, searching for another spot. We found it, and all was well. Then, on another trip on the Tennessee Buffalo with George Grider, Lydel Sims, Jack Ramsay, and a couple of others, Jack was my bow paddle. We were fishing with fly rods for bream. One of us, Jack or me, hooked a tree limb. Jack began to untangle it. A snake dropped into the bow, almost in his lap. Jack never tired of retelling that story, how he did *not* capsize the boat but retreated backward and ultimately, somehow, got the snake back out of the boat.

In 1961 or 1962, Lucius Burch founded a lunch group, the Wolf River Society for the Prevention of Taking Oneself Too Seriously. I was vice president of that club in its first year. (It's now known as the Wolf River Club. Most people aren't familiar with the former name.) It was a nice group. It met upstairs at a place on Madison between Second and Third Streets. It's up a long flight of stairs. We had the same cook for many, many years: Mamie. I imagine she's gone to her grave by now. The general idea was that you would arrive and you'd take an empty seat. One day you'd be talking with these guys and the next day with those guys. Well, Wynn Smith and his little crowd, they didn't like it that way. This little clique of conservatives rode roughshod over the unwritten rules. They always were going to sit at the same table and always going to talk to each other. They had a club within a club. From my point of view, that was the beginning of a downhill slide.

Meeman's retirement in 1962 left me badly placed, a "teacher's pet" with no teacher. The new executive editor—leave him nameless—was no match for Meeman, and did not stay with Meeman's principles. I endured it, having no place to go. But a phone call came one day from Washington. My friend George Grider, who had won a seat on our County Commission (then known as the County Quarterly Court) in 1960, had with the help of black voters now won a seat in the Ninth Congressional District. He was calling to ask me if I would like to be assistant director of the U.S. Commission on Civil Rights' Mid-South office. I couldn't have been more delighted.

Chapter Nineteen

A Crisis of Black and White

Aside from my reporting, I was also becoming involved in community affairs. In the early Fifties we had a Better Schools Committee. We integrated the membership and held meetings, which included blacks and whites, in my home. Not all of our efforts were well received. Visits to my home by people with black skin led to our children being ostracized by the other neighborhood children. Their parents would say, "Don't you play with those Spence children. They're Communists." I was ashamed of those neighbors. They had college educations, and you would have thought they would have been broader minded. The Communist notion was still affecting people in those days.

Racial integration in Memphis, Tennessee did not come from our being kind hearted. It came under the force of law. There was a lot of foot dragging. Many people never changed their minds. I might be one of them. I think I have some racial prejudice. It's partly a matter of class, and partly carryover from those days when whites felt paternal and maternal. We felt kindly toward the blacks, but we thought of them as children. We laughed at them a lot, among ourselves. We also admired their good nature, their humor, their music, and their care for each other.

In 1965, I joined the staff of the U.S. Commission on Civil Rights. My friend Congressman George Grider wanted to bring the office to Memphis and to get credit for it. He needed my help to get it here. George and I had become great friends by that time. I had campaigned hard for him. We were hunting and fishing companions. He was one of my best friends for the rest of his life. So I was pleased to be asked to help start the local office of the Civil Rights Commission.

The commission was not an enforcement agency; it was a watchdog agency concerned with educating the public. We had what we called advisory committees. The committee members were unusually able persons. Almost all were professional or business people of high standing in their communities, and they were courageous, prominent people—blacks and whites—in every state. From the black community, we had mainly black doctors and black hairdressers, people with secure positions. Nobody was going to fire them from their jobs, so they could take a public stand for civil rights. They were grand people. We had courageous white people serving as well. Some suffered harassment, including a college president. Some Mississippi planters were also courageous enough to stand up.

I served with the commission from 1965 to 1969. As assistant director of the Southern Field Office, my job was to act as the liaison for these advisory committees. My primary territory was Mississippi, Arkansas, and Tennessee. I also covered Oklahoma, Missouri, Texas, and Washington, D.C. Our director was Jacques Wilmore, a black man. Wilmore was a graduate of Swarthmore College, run by Quakers, and had recently been with the Peace Corps in Nigeria. We had four blacks and two whites in the Memphis office. The other white was a young woman, a secretary. She was very capable, and worked easily with a well-qualified black woman, Rosetta Miller. Bobby Doctor was the other person working as liaison with our state committees of volunteers.

We encouraged people to vote. There was still a lot of intimidation and lack of familiarity with the process. One effect of our meetings was to bring people together to organize, or be aware that there were people out there trying to make things better. I would find a federal building, if there was one, as a meeting place, or a hotel with an assembly hall.

Of course there was hostility. People were either for us or against us. Many were against us.

Much of what we did was symbolic. Years earlier, when Mayor Tobey began to indicate his independence from Mr. Crump, he would accompany me on a walk down Main Street on the way to lunch. Little things like that. Later I probably was the first person to take a black to lunch with the Wolf River Club. That happened when I took my boss, Jacques Wilmore. I think his attendance at the lunch drove away at least one member.

From 1927 through 1954, the heyday of Boss Crump, Memphis whites moved at a snail's pace toward integration of schools, restaurants, and other public facilities. Elsewhere, the civil rights movement had been making headway. In the 1930s, the NAACP's lawyers, both black and white, began to win cases in the Federal courts. Thurgood Marshall and Jack Greenberg were the leading lawyers. But as early as 1952 in Memphis—before the landmark *Brown v. Board of Education* ruling that struck down school segregation—Vasco and Maxine Smith, Jimmy Walker, a union leader, and his wife, Ms. Willa McWilliams Walker, were meeting privately with four whites who had distinguished themselves as liberals eager to see equality between the races. These men were Lydel Sims, newspaper columnist; George Grider, then still a lawyer; our friend Jim Draper, who later served on the U.S. Community Relations Service (CRS) staff; and me. I was invited to join the group, the Memphis Committee on Community Relations (MCCR), because I had just written the series of articles exposing the inequality between black and white county schools.

As we moved forward, six black Memphians led the way: Maxine and Vasco Smith, Russell B. Sugarmon Jr.,[16] Judge Ben Hooks, and A. W. Willis, and Jesse Turner.[17] Sugarmon, Willis, and Hooks were young lawyers. Their office was in the NAACP Building on Vance Avenue. They startled white Memphians in 1959 by playing a major role in that year's city elections. As I remember, Russell Sugarmon ran for a seat on the five-man Public Works Commission, and there was consternation among whites at the thought that he might win. Whites ganged up behind Bill Farris, and Sugarmon lost, but from there on everyone knew that there was a new force to be reckoned with in Memphis politics. Maxine and Vasco Smith became public figures the next year, 1960, as they recruited and trained young black youths, male and female, to stage successful sit-ins at downtown lunch counters, which often led to their arrest. More than a hundred went to jail on one occasion. As a reporter, I was there.

In the MCCR, I served with such wonderful men as Hollis F. Price, Le Moyne College president; the Rev. J.A. McDaniel, Taylor Hays, owner of the funeral home his father had founded; and Edwin Dalstrom, a white businessman and Boy Scout leader. I think Dalstrom and I were the only whites on the board over time.

What I mainly did while traveling for the Civil Rights Commission was organize public meetings throughout the Mid-South region. Our mission was to convince folks that it was time to change. Many attended. We didn't spend much effort planning, but we got good media coverage. What we were up against was decades of prejudice and segregation.

I did a lot of driving. Those were the years civil rights workers were being killed. One night I thought someone was following me, so I sped up, and after a time the car fell back and disappeared. Of course, I might have imagined it all; I never was threatened in person, nor did I ever receive any threatening letters.

We did set out to talk directly to Mayor Loeb about fairness in city government. I wrote a very carefully couched, diplomatic letter to the mayor and his new City Fire and Police Commissioner, Frank Holloman, saying that we, the Southern Field Office, wanted to discuss the behavior of the city police. This was in January or February of 1968. We wanted to talk about the number of black officers on the force, their seniority, the assignments to squad cars and to neighborhoods, the techniques of patrolling. This was all within the context of the civil rights of the blacks. We would have talked about courtesy titles and treatment of people in jail and their allegations of brutality, what sort of training the police ought to have and who ought to give it, what resources we thought were available to him that he might not be using for training, and the recruitment of officers.

Another continuing concern was over the fire department and the lack of integration in its ranks. There were too few promotions. For a long time there had been a separate segregated fire company: black firemen and white firemen slept in separate dormitories and ate out of different kitchens. We recognized the absurdity—and possible danger to the public safety—of enforcing this division. We felt there was room for improvement. We were volunteering whatever help we could give to a man whom we thought wanted all the help he could get. But the meeting with Holloman never came off.

On February 1, 1968, two sanitation workers were killed on the job when, seeking shelter from the cold and rain, they had crawled into the bay of a garbage truck. Because the two workers were black, they weren't allowed under the shed where the white workers were shielding themselves from the elements. Lightning activated the compactor's hydraulic ram, crushing both of the black men. The newspapers failed to report the tragic accident in the same light as the death of two white policemen killed in the line of duty might have been.

On February 12, the Memphis sanitation workers called up a strike. Since the 1930s, labor's struggles to unionize in the South had been met by hostility and outright defeat. In August 1966, Memphis sanitation workers had voted to strike, but a court injunction threatening arrests and an ample supply of scabs ended the strike before it started. The city's black middle class was never behind the union. But this time it was different. A week or so later, on

February 23, 1968, strikers and their supporters marched downtown. The workers wanted better working conditions, and more than that, they wanted recognition, they wanted a union, one the city would recognize and that would be empowered to collect workers' dues.

That morning the city council had met to consider a new resolution that gave the strikers, in essence, what they'd been asking for—namely a recognized, fully functional union along with a pay raise. It had been approved in committee. The seat of the Memphis government had by now become a tinderbox. In attendance were about a thousand people, mostly black. Police were everywhere. On this day, the audience was hoping for good news. After hours of debate, the council returned a watered down resolution, one whose points had already been approved by Mayor Loeb but fell far short of the strikers' demands. Outraged citizens spontaneously marched from City Hall to Mason Temple, long the site of civil rights activities in Memphis.

The march would become known as the "Macing on Main Street." Police were roughing up the participants, spraying them up close with mace. One victim was my boss, Jacques Wilmore. On that day I happened to be in Greenwood, Mississippi. I learned about the police violence late that night when Mary Ann called. I sat down right away and made a number of telephone calls to Memphis. Strike leaders mailed night letters to several hundred black ministers. When you wanted action in the black community, you notified the ministers.

The first thing I did the next day on getting back to Memphis was to set up a meeting for the following day with members of the MCCR. The group had been around since the 1950s and it had gotten results, modest maybe and less than people like Dr. Vasco Smith, Billy Kyles, and Reverend Jim Lawson normally expect; but it had been a very useful thing.

As one of the committee's early members, I was in an ideal position to organize this meeting. This was my job, to bring people together, to set up meetings. In this case, we needed an umbrella group to bring together the many organizations that were trying to affect change in Memphis. Ed Orgill was the first person I called. I thought he could help form the organization's base. If I were going to get Orgill to come—and frankly it didn't matter much whether he was there or not—at least I wanted him to know that I was after a bilateral power structure: a white power structure and black power structure. I wanted them to get face to face. Hollis Price of Lemoyne Owen College was there because I wanted his facility. When you ask a man if you can use his place you usually invite him to join in. Dr. Price had a position not of power, but of influence. As I had learned years earlier, there's a difference.

I avoided inviting the union people. I felt that Ned Cook could talk with his close friend the mayor, and Lawson and Turner would talk with Jerry Wurf. (Wurf, president of the American Federation of State, County, and Municipal Employees, or AFSCME, lived in New York and was presently not in town anyway.) I didn't think it was important to have Bill Lucy, the AFSCME associate director.

The Black Organizing Project—a grassroots group of college students modeled loosely on the Black Panthers—were an undercurrent during these initial meetings with established civil rights organizers. Known informally as the Invaders, they indeed had the effect of keeping the establishment—black and white—at the negotiating table. Sometimes we didn't know what to make of them, nor they of us.

After spending the morning of February 24 organizing the meeting for the next day, I went over to Mason Temple where the ministers were arriving for today's meeting. It was clear right away they wanted action. The first order of business was formulating a name for the new organization: we chose the Committee on the Move for Equality, or COME. Jim Lawson came up with it. A nationally prominent civil rights activist, a Memphis minister, and a close associate of Dr. King, Lawson was also elected chairman.

We met in a large conference room. Some twenty-odd people were there that first day, including Baxton Bryant, and three of us from the commission's office: Bobby Doctor, Mrs. Miller, and myself. Also Mrs. Cornelia Crenshaw, Mrs. Matthews, and the ministers attended, including Rev. Henry Starks. Starks was in almost every meeting I attended. Mrs. Crenshaw had been a strike supporter from the beginning and was outspoken. You might say she was militant. There was some understanding that perhaps she had a constituency, though it was undefined. I didn't stay for that meeting, because I was working on the one I'd planned for the next day. Other meetings I missed because I had to return to Mississippi to continue my work.

The next day, Sunday, February 25, we held the emergency meeting of the Memphis Committee on Community Relations. Our plan was to discuss the growing turmoil. About twelve of us sat in the LeMoyne College faculty lounge. Wilmore and I were there representing the Commission on Civil Rights, along with Dr. Hollis Price, and three or four city councilmen. These included Louis Donelson, Wyeth Chandler, and Downing Pryor, and perhaps Jerred Blanchard. Also attending were Jim Lawson, Jesse Turner (now president of the local NAACP chapter), Burt Ferguson (the white owner of a black radio station, WDIA), Carl Carson, Ned Cook, and two or three others. Chandler attended at the request of one of the black leaders; I believe it was Lawson. Neither Arthur McCain, former president of the Union Planters National Bank, nor Ed Orgill were present.

Every person there knew me and had known me a long time. There's no substitute for a long or an intimate acquaintance when you're bringing people together. I found this true when I came to Memphis from Chattanooga as a newspaperman. Then I found myself competing with an old-hand reporter. He would beat me to a story simply because he knew people; it's easy to talk to people you know. Everybody in this de facto group was on a first-name basis or quickly adopted that mode of address.

As the meeting began, I told them, the white people particularly, that what we had was a crisis and that it was a crisis of black and white; it wasn't simply a labor union problem.

This was important because whenever I finally managed to reach Ed Orgill and Arthur McClain, both of them insisted that it was a labor/management issue. And they were very much opposed to the city recognizing a union. McCain said, "We can manage without having unions." He was drawing on his experience as a banker and as a city father in White Plains, New York. I replied that the strike was symbolic to Memphis blacks. It was a racial matter any way you cut it. Virtually all of the striking workers were black. The Memphis power structure was white. No white workers in the city would be expected to endure the abysmal pay and working conditions of the sanitation workers—just as no white children in the city schools would be expected to use outdoor toilets. Thus it was far more important to solve the racial problem than it was to stand on a principle of not negotiating with unions. McCain and others were hung up with the law; they said the law was written such that we couldn't negotiate. Even if they had been right, they would have been wrong. Later they were proved wrong on both counts.

The MCCR meeting was friendly. There was a consensus, you might say. Everybody in the room thought that two or three simple things could resolve the problem, though we also scheduled a follow-up meeting in early March. Ned Cook was to draft a letter to Mayor Loeb and Jerry Wurf, the national president of the American Federation of State, County, and Municipal Employees (AFSCME), which I believe did get written. The text was based on something that Loeb had already written and issued. Ned was going to say, "Now you do this, Henry, and Wurf will do this, and we will settle this thing." We discussed what these two or three issues were. We were telling each other what we thought was the most we could get from Wurf and the most we could get from Loeb. And we said, "Well, if we get this from each of them, that's it."

It was going to be a pretty fast-moving thing. Those in charge moved quickly, but it just didn't come off.

The next day, February 26, the COME organizers held a march, the first of a series of daily marches. As with all the marches, the makeup was overwhelmingly black and there were a lot of people. The weather was cold as we left from Clayborn Temple. Rev. Starks led the march, walking slowly down Main Street in front of the marchers, making certain that the rules for the march were observed. This was one of those events where you kept a certain interval and you stopped for the lights and obeyed all the rules. It was new to him and new to a lot of the marchers. Policemen were standing all along the route. I was moving about, doing whatever I could to make it clear to anyone that I was an official observer.

Starks had been maced in the Macing on Main Street; today he was nervous and cold. I'd been walking beside him a little while. I said, "You're cold. Let me go get you some coffee." I ran into the Claridge Hotel and picked up some hot coffee in paper cups, and we chatted along.

When the march turned around at city hall, there was a middle-aged, rather poorly dressed white man who yelled something. The man said nothing obscene, nor did he disturb the peace exactly. But he couldn't contain himself and had to shout something like, "smart aleck," or "nigger," or something like that. And this was the sort of thing that every man in the march had been expecting at any moment from any white person standing along the whole long line. Movement was slow and it took about an hour and a half to complete the march, but it all went peacefully.

On March 5, there was a sit-in held in the city council chambers. Hundreds of people participated. I was back in Memphis from my work in Mississippi that day, and observed the one hundred or more demonstrators getting arrested. I was particularly interested in the fact that it seemed every black policeman in the city was assigned that particular duty. It seemed a bit ironic. It was as if they said, "Well, if somebody's got to arrest all these black people, let's let it be black policemen." They formed a cordon in the aisle, and they marched the demonstrators out across the street. I followed them into the jail and saw the line-up and the photographing and the whole process.

During the demonstration, I saw Maxine Smith and joked with her. Maxine was the Director for the Memphis NAACP and a zealous civil rights organizer. You didn't mess with Maxine. Later I overheard that when she was in custody she was sent in to the men's toilet.

The next day, March 6, I attended a hearing (in Municipal Court) where charges were dropped against most of the protestors. I talked with some of the union leaders and with members of the city council. That afternoon in Chancery Court, I watched Judge Hoffman hit the strike leaders hard, awarding them jail time and steep fines for contempt of court for violating his order prohibiting strike activities.

I happened to be sitting behind Mayor Loeb. He turned around and looked, and I looked at him without smiling or anything, just met his eyes.

He said, "What's the matter?"

"I don't think things are going very well. I don't like what's happening."

"Nobody does!" Then he stuck his hand out and we shook hands and that was it.

On March 7, Wurf gave an outstanding presentation to the city council. I think the council was impressed. The council was considering councilmember Rev. Patterson's proposal for allowing the union "dues-checkoff," considered crucial for union viability. This had been one of the key stumbling blocks during negotiations. All along, I had thought any solution to the strike might have to be through the council. I counted ahead and there were six sure votes. These included the three black councilmen: Reverend J. L. Netters, Reverend J. O. Patterson, and Fred Davis. The whites in our camp were Pryor, Blanchard, and Donelson. I'd talked with others about it. We thought maybe if we could get the necessary seven votes …

"Who's number seven?" we asked. "Will it be Gwen Awsumb?"

"No, not right now," someone said. "She's in Mexico City." So we were stuck on six, and with only six we weren't getting anywhere. How could we break the deadlock? Predictably, the council voted Patterson's proposal down. It seemed like things were only getting worse.

On the morning of March 8, as planned, the MCCR held its follow-up meeting at LeMoyne College. Most of the same people (including the city councilmen) were there. This time Ed Orgill was there, and he presided. Frank Miles and Maxine Smith, who also had missed the February 25 meeting, were there. That made about twelve of us. Downing Pryor was there, Blanchard, I believe, surely was there. I'm not sure whether Billy Kyles was there. Chandler was not, nor was Wilmore.

By this time, the so-called Donelson Resolution on Equal Employment Opportunity for the city had been proposed and made public. Louis Donelson had drafted an affirmative-action program for upper-level city jobs. This would naturally open these jobs to blacks. The council had discussed it but failed to adopt it.

Frank Miles was a labor leader and close associate of Mayor Loeb. We had him there to talk about the problems of a union and management. He took the side of the union, speaking as a former union member, leader, and mediator, and was more an advocate in this informal meeting than he could have been publicly. Possibly he was in negotiations with the city. Frank was a stranger to some of the black leaders who were there, such as Jim Lawson. I won't say he was a stranger to Jesse Turner because Turner knew everybody, but I think in this meeting we began with some people using "Mr. Miles" and it ended up with them calling him Frank. He was talking mainly to Lawson, Turner, and Maxine Smith.

A disturbing event happened that day that might easily have unraveled any progress we were making. A reporter for the *Press-Scimitar* somehow learned about the meeting. As a former reporter myself, I thought the more power to her. But keep in mind all of this had to be kept private, at least until agreements could be reached; I'd been saying the meeting was private and it was understood there'd be no reporters present. I don't know where she got her lead, but she did a good job of nosing up the stairs and trying to buttonhole somebody who stepped out to go to the bathroom. She was there ready to quiz us once the meeting was over. Ed Orgill got on the telephone and called Charlie Schneider, the editor of the *Press-Scimitar*. Ed said, "Don't put anything in the paper about this meeting," and Schneider honored that request. As things turned out, that meeting had no concrete results anyway.

I had to return to Greenwood to continue working on the Mississippi project, and I was out of town during most of the next two weeks. The eminent black American who had inspired the nation five years earlier by telling of his dream for America's racial healing, Martin Luther King Jr. himself appeared in Memphis on March 18 to rally the strikers, as newspapers were claiming the strike was failing. That night he spoke before a jubilant crowd of seventeen thousand at Mason Temple. At one point he called for a citywide strike, thrilling his audience of thousands and sending shock waves through the white community.

On March 28, we held the granddaddy of the marches, to be led by Martin Luther King Jr., who was flying in that morning from Atlanta. In recent months, King had identified poverty as a civil rights issue and started working tirelessly on his plans for a Poor People's Campaign; he and his staff had seen the Memphis strike as a key opportunity for pressuring whites and giving a break to the poor. On this day, we all were hoping this great man, who espoused Gandhi's nonviolent teachings, would lead not only a peaceful march, but also a productive one.

I began the day with Charles Poole, a member of the Tennessee State Advisory Committee for the Commission on Civil Rights. As we walked down Main Street toward the head of the march, we observed the scarcity of police and remarked on it. "Where are they?" We saw fewer that morning than during any of the daily marches down Main Street. "Why aren't they here?"

Poole and I arrived early at the Clayborn Temple, the center for the strikers and the planners. The day was sunny and starting to get warm. It felt like a homecoming for many of us. We saw people we knew and shook their hands; we'd see someone we hadn't expected to see and were pleased. There would be somebody with his wife and his kids, and here would be a fellow from Atlanta or Washington. We'd say, "Hello, nice to see you."

Early on I became concerned, as many did, about how slowly the march was starting, and how unmanageable it was insofar as keeping the people in the street. There was a press of people. Still, good humor prevailed—at least until the rumor about Hamilton High came in. At Hamilton High School that morning, we heard, Memphis police had tear-gassed students who had assembled their own march, moving toward downtown. A number were hurt. There must have been mothers and fathers or brothers and sisters of the Hamilton students around me. People were saying, "That's too bad. I wonder what's going on out there."

It was unsettling and disturbing news, and everyone had in the pit of his stomach the idea that a crisis was in the making. This was the ever-present trouble whenever blacks confronted authority. "Are we going to be able to do this? Are we not going to be beat over the head? Are we going to have a safe return?" This was what was on one's mind. No exodus occurred from the march area, though. Nor did I see people queuing up to the phone booth or dashing into the Minimum Salary Building to get to a telephone. At some point a contingent arrived from some school, maybe even from Hamilton High.

Still we were delayed. It got on to be eleven o'clock and there were the usual rumors about whether Dr. King was going to get there and where he was.

Someone said, "He's landed at the airport, he's coming."

There were protest signs. Many were aimed at Loeb, calling him "King Henry." There was a "Horse's Ass" sign. There may have been something like "Henry Loeb God Damn." There was the ubiquitous "I am a Man" sign. The ministers were trying to maintain order and decorum and whether they would have censored a sign I don't know, but I didn't see any real vulgarity. I thought about how the sticks could be considered as potential weapons. I had my son right beside me, and I never let him out of my sight. My daughter, a senior at Central High school, was somewhere in the throng. She and a classmate Rosaline Willis, A. W. Willis' daughter, were in this great crowd and I had a fatherly concern about my daughter's whereabouts.

I stepped into the Clayborn Temple to see who was there. John Smith and some others were haranguing a group of young people. It was a small group, perhaps several dozen. I won't say that they were teenagers; that may be too precise. The first five or six or eight rows of pews were fairly well filled. A young black man saw me and watched as I moved slowly in. He came up to me and said, "You don't belong in here, you've got to get out." A black minister—I don't remember which one—had observed my entry. He said to the young man, "This is a church. Anyone is welcome here." The young man returned to his seat.

Reverend Smith was saying that marches and demonstrations don't get the job done. "There's too much talk," he was saying. "These old fogies leading this thing . . . we're tired of following them." I don't believe he made any overt or direct statement like "Swing those sticks." I did not hear any incitement to violence. A night or two before, in the same Clayborn Temple, there had been a big meeting, and the Invaders had distributed their Molotov cocktail recipe. They were permitted to do this. I'm sure there were ministers present who didn't like its being done, but they didn't stop them. It was considered an issue of freedom of speech.

I stayed only long enough to establish the fact that I wasn't leaving simply because I was ordered out, no matter what. Outside, I quickly joined the march, which had now begun to move.

I became aware that King had arrived. I went to the front of the march only to see the problem of getting him in place with people beside him and rooting him on. Then I thought it was better for me to be farther back. I stayed about a hundred yards behind King, not even in sight of him. I was with Walter Bailey. Walter's wife and child were five yards away. He had his concern about his wife and his child, who was quite young. I saw Harold Whalum. I saw Billy Kyles.

We were between Third and Second on Beale when we heard the first breaking of glass. This just chilled me completely. I couldn't exactly locate it. I didn't see it and couldn't know what caused it to break, but it was a chilling kind of thing. "Oh Lord," I wondered. "Is something bad about to happen? What is happening? Who's doing this?" Somebody in the crowd made a comment: "This ought not to happen," or "That's bad." The crowd had been an orderly crowd. They wanted an orderly march. Most were adults. Then teenagers ran by, and at some point sticks were thrown. I had been concerned about the teenagers because they are exuberant and irreverent, and they like to taunt the authorities, whether they're schoolteachers, mommas and poppas, or police.

Somewhere between Main and Second I heard people shouting. "Turn around, go back to Clayborn Temple, go back to Clayborn Temple, back to Clayborn Temple." Many were shouting. People picked it up. "Okay, our party's over; somebody spoiled it." People had a resentful, exasperated reaction that this major effort, this buildup, this cost of emotion was all going to waste. The march would have to be turned around and sent back. "It's a mighty shame that this is being broken up" was the general feeling. There wasn't any resistance to going back once people got the word. Most were glad to disassociate themselves as quickly as they could from this law breaking.

We started back. I was afraid of two things: first, that people would become panic-stricken and run back and crush each other, or possibly overrun a child or girl or Marty Spence. I still didn't know where she was. Because the march was a family affair, many in the crowd were in the same condition. People had brought their children along so that they could say in later years, "I marched with Dr. Martin Luther King in Memphis when I was five years old." Or "I marched," or "My wife was there."

I lost Dr. King in the march and wouldn't see him until later. We had no information about what he was doing.

A few marchers began to run. Of course, there were people who could run faster than other people, particularly the teenagers. They began to fill the sidewalks. With the retreat, the effort to vandalize grew. Maybe some teenagers who hadn't thought they were going to do anything illegal or violent decided otherwise. "Well, it's over and the police are forcing us back and making us run." They resented having to retreat and they began throwing things.

I was standing at Hernando and Beale when I saw the break-in of the liquor store there, the looting of it, the going in, the taking of liquor, the passing out of bottles, and the drinking of liquor all on the spot, and all very fast. These were probably men in their twenties. Feet and clubs were used and I remember thinking how tough the glass was, and it took a few raps. First one and then several men; I'd say it was a gang thing, but whether the members of the gang had been a gang before the event, or simply joined immediately and were partners thereof, I don't know. If you're going to loot and you want approval and assistance, anybody who joins you is with you. There was also the third element, the drifter element and, by golly, free liquor is just something you don't pass up.

Others have speculated that the window-breakers and then the looters were different people. I think this is true. I believe there was a wild throwing of clubs, or sticks, by people who maybe didn't intend to loot but just decided to break windows. I don't think it was two people saying, "Let's break it in and then let's go in." They just said, "Let's break." And then having broken and it was open, "Well, gosh," and then somebody else would say, "I'll go in." And since some of the sticks were thrown from across the street, the person separated from the plate glass window by a whole lot of people obviously had no intention of looting himself, not personally.

The police were moving up from behind. I was very much aware of the fact that they were back there, and I remember wondering if they were on foot, car, or horse, and what they'd have on. I remember seeing gas masks. I had a more vivid impression as they approached south on Hernando, this line of fearful-looking men in gas masks and with clubs and shotguns and so on.

These were Memphis city police. I don't remember seeing any sheriff's deputies at that time. So far, there wasn't any contact between the police and marchers. Harold Whalum stood in the street telling people to take it easy. I remember thinking how pretty he looked, so neatly dressed as he always was. I remember seeing Maxine Smith upstairs at the NAACP office. I kept on moving because I was thinking as much about Marty as I was about observing and doing my official duty. I reached the Minimum Salary Building and Clayborn Temple, then left there and started to make my way, still on foot, to the Federal Building to get a car.

I was walking down Hernando Street. There had been an advance by a row of policemen from Third Street moving east on Pontotoc, a line abreast, ordering people off the street and into their houses; there are a few houses on Pontotoc between Third and Hernando. And the police would say, "Get in your houses, get off the porch, inside," and police would rush at them. And this was loud and rough, maybe necessarily so. It certainly wasn't calculated to soothe anybody's feelings. I tried to tell the police, "Take it easy, take it easy, you don't have to be so brusque." I don't think I used that word.

I was in my usual business dress, coat and tie, and I had my credential on me. As I got near the corner of Pontotoc and Hernando I encountered a police officer. He was saying, "Who are you and why are you having anything to say?" And, "Are you with these people? Have you been here all along?" I didn't know just why that was relevant.

"I've been with this thing from the start."

"You ought to be with them. Go on, get with them." He shoved me forcibly. I don't know whether he swung a club on me or not, but he didn't hit me. Then he pulled out his mace can and squirted me in the face. Glasses are a good protection against mace, so my eyes were not really hurt. I was blinded for no more than a few seconds.

"All right, you're one of them," he said, after he saw my credentials.

This was a repeat of what had happened to Jacques Wilmore on the February 23 march. I decided it was time to go to Commissioner Holloman's office. This would be my first visit there since this all began. I went not to protest my macing necessarily, but to ask Holloman what he was doing and how we could help. I found him in a state of agitation, and understandably so. Standing before him, with the police and the marchers outside, I mentioned that I had been maced.

"No you weren't," he said. I felt that the matter wasn't worth arguing over. I could only think that he meant that I had been tear-gassed, not maced. When I asked what he was doing in response to the situation, he said he was calling for the National Guard. "No one gave me a line of march; I haven't had any communication with these people. I've had to play this by ear and I do the best I can."

At the mayor's office, I was told Loeb was not in the building. This was about twelve o'clock so he was probably out to lunch. I don't have any reason to doubt whatever I was told because I talked with Jerry Jackson and Jerry was an old acquaintance. I also telephoned my home, and my Washington office. I told them that all hell had broken loose in Memphis.

By this time I was accompanied by Mike Cody, an associate with Lucius Burch's firm. I'd picked him up outside his office on Second Street. "You ought to go with me now," I said. Mike and I got in my car and went back down to Clayborn Temple. At around 12:30 or afterward, we parked on Pontotoc Avenue in back of the film warehouse. There we observed the continuing battle at Clayborn Temple and the Minimum Salary Building. David Caywood was standing outside and I was hanging to the side of the building because someone was throwing objects from the Minimum Salary porch.

Both buildings were under siege. Police stood north and south of the intersection and the entrances. Nearby a man named Seward, a black man, sat in a pickup truck. (I don't remember his first name. I had met him earlier in connection with the shooting of James Meredith.) His truck had flat tires; it wasn't going anywhere. It was a service station pickup, as I remember. He had a loudspeaker and he was yelling things at both parties trying to make the peace. His truck was parked ten yards or so from the entrance to the Minimum Salary Building, and the same distance from the north door of Clayborn Temple. I remember thinking, "I wish I had your nerve."

The police had tear gas and/or shotguns. Though I did not actually see them fire tear gas into either building, I did see smudge on the baseboard where a canister smoldered. One canister was fired from a launcher across the street. This was not the first canister I had seen fired. I saw Jerred Blanchard and another friend, both of whom had their eyes streaming, probably from the tear gas. It seems that the bystanders are always the ones who catch it the worst.

Around two o'clock or a little later, I finally learned that my daughter was safe, thus allowing me to tend to business. I went into the office of the film company and made some calls. I had lost Cody somehow and I decided that I should go to the Rivermont Hotel where I'd learned Dr. King was staying.

Later we learned that a sixteen-year-old black boy had been shot and killed that day by a white policeman. The police would claim the boy was shot in self-defense, reporting he'd brandished a pistol. The police were never able to produce the alleged weapon but the grand jury declined to indict the officer.

Perhaps Dr. King and the Southern Christian Leadership Council had been expecting too much. Even though a great majority of the marchers had followed King's philosophy of nonviolence on that hopeful day, it took only a few troublemakers to ruin it. Plans would soon be made for a second march, but first we had to clean up the damage. And we had to calm the city.

Chapter Twenty

The Angels Weren't With Us

That evening, on March 28, I went to Dr. King's suite in the Rivermont Hotel, where I saw two or three people I knew. I introduced myself to a couple more I hadn't met, men from New York City and another from Memphis. Billy Kyles was there. He was important in the Committee on the Move for Equality, a committee chair in the NAACP, and also a member of our Tennessee Advisory Committee. This made it easy for us to call on each other for help. Jim Lawson was there at some point. Probably Harold Middlebrook was around. Autry Parker, director of MAP-South, was there.

I wasn't the sort of person who would be invited into the inner sanctum, that being Dr. King's bedroom. My status was tenuous. Was I wanted or wasn't I wanted? And was there any hostility there? Young militants whom I didn't know—though I knew who they were—were standing around. Charles Cabbage might have been there.

You couldn't say how many there were because people came and went. A considerable number were in and out. Many would go into Dr. King's bedroom. Primarily, I was glad to know that he was there. I think this was why I went there in the first place. His safety was important. I also wanted to learn from those who would decide what the next move was. Would there be a march the next day? Would there be statements? Did they want me to serve in any liaison capacity?

In the hotel lobby I called my Washington office again and my office in the Federal Building in Memphis. "I'm here, this is what's going on. These are the people who are here. Any suggestions?" I asked if I should take a room here and set up headquarters. It was agreed I would.

About four o'clock someone came out of Dr. King's room. It might have been Jim Lawson or Billy Kyles, someone from the COME leadership. Henry Starks might have been there. They said, "We wondered if we can get on the air quickly with a message for the public to stay home, and let's have no violence."

"I think I can swing something, let me make a call." I decided to call Frank Ahlgren at the *Commercial Appeal.*

"Frank, I've got to have all three television stations down here in thirty minutes. Can you get them here?"

"Well, you know, John, we don't have anything to do with WMCT anymore."

"I know that, Frank, but we got to have them."

"OK, I'll get them."

Time was a factor. I wanted Frank's power and I wanted his switchboard. I put it in his hands. I didn't care how he did it; if he wanted three people making three simultaneous calls, great.

I went to the desk and said, "I'm John Spence, U.S. Commission on Civil Rights, and I've got to have a conference room. Will you give it to me?"

"What's it for?"

"We're going to have a press conference."

"They told us they don't want any publicity."

"Well, they do. They want it now."

This began with a clerk, but soon I was talking with the hotel manager. "I'll be accountable for the expense, bill it to me." I didn't bother to ask what the room would cost. I believe it cost $40, which was a bit steep.

By now the word was definite that at five o'clock they would have a press conference in the Rivermont. Dr. King and several of his people would be there, and a script had been prepared. And by five o'clock, there were twenty or thirty people on camera and an equal number in the room who were watching, not including the several cameras and any number of station personnel—in just forty-five minutes, people not only got the word but got themselves to the Rivermont. It was agreed that all these people would flank Dr. King. They were people who wanted to be there and they were going to be in the act. I think Jesse Turner was there and took part, Maxine and Vasco, and, of course, Lawson. This was taped and they got it on the air fairly promptly. I don't think they made the six o'clock news with it, but they came to do the best they could and as quickly as they could. It was quite interesting that everything proceeded as fast as it did.

I went to my room and tried to catch my breath. I had called several people and told them that we had this room, they were free to use it. Billy Kyles was one of these. We turned on the television and saw the CBS six o'clock news with Walter Cronkite. He showed the Memphis police beating people.

We had supper that night in the Rivermont restaurant. "How do we get out of this place with a curfew on?" Kyles asked. Keep in mind that Kyles was black.

"You better go with me," I said. We were to pick up Jacques Wilmore, who was coming in from Birmingham. At around 7:00 p.m., we drove to the airport and took him to his home. We saw a few National Guard trucks, not much traffic otherwise. There were more cars in the white neighborhoods than in the black. I got home that night; I never slept in that room at the Rivermont.

At home, I learned that the Central High school principal had suspended my daughter Marty, along with Rosaline Willis and Reverend W. Williamson's daughter Gwen, and whoever else might have participated in the march—for missing school, or playing hooky, as it was also described.

I spent most of my nights, from March 28 on, attending COME strategy meetings. Driving to and from home, I was never stopped. I didn't roam the whole city; I was usually downtown. One night in particular, I remember taking a young fellow named Tommy Green, a teenager, home to extreme North Memphis. The house in which he lived faced the Wolf River levee; it's up in the Douglass neighborhood and I remember thinking I'd better take him home if he was going to get there. I made no effort to follow the police or listen to the police radio or anything.

The next day, Friday the 29th, I drove over to the Board of Education first thing in the morning. There I made my case. "My daughter was absent with my consent," I explained, pointing out that the march was as educational and useful as other events children are often excused for. "I want her back in school."

"OK, she can return to school. You go to Central High and see the principal Bob King." I can't remember who I was talking with. We knew each other, likely on account of my friendship with Frances Coe, a member of the school board.

"I want this to apply to the other children too," I added.

I went to see Bob King. Mr. King hadn't gotten the word I was coming. He was a little stuffy. He didn't say, "Oh sure, send her on back." So I had to pursue that. The last person I talked to was Harry Sharp. Harry said, "Oh, yeah, sure, John." He was quite sensible about it.

My ire was based on the fact that the principal was suspending a child for a one day's absence despite knowing the child was acting with his or her parent's permission. He also knew what the absent child was doing, which I'm certain made a difference in his attitude. Certainly no one said, "Y'all did a good thing." Some of the children had difficulties missing tests or homework, which Marty, fortunately, was able to avoid. It all happened so fast.

This chore accomplished, I returned to my office. It seemed like everyone was having a meeting. I acted as a liaison between the various factions. The union was having a meeting at the Rubber Workers' building and COME may have been meeting as well. Dr. King was somewhere else. One group was planning to do one thing and another was planning to do another. I was afraid that each group, not knowing what the other one was going to do, would have something conflicting to say. My job was to say to one group, "Did you know that so-and-so was going to do this?"

"Well no, I didn't."

"That's going to make some difference in our plans. I better get on the telephone."

At my office, I also compared statements from the respective press conferences to ensure they were in agreement. And I met with the group planning another march for that afternoon. The leaders discussed participation and nonviolence.

"This will be limited to adults."

"Who's an adult?" someone asked. There was some trouble with a group of young men who had the Black Power look: natural hair, dashikis, and informal dress. We had some trouble, but I didn't follow that from start to finish. The march on the 28th produced the famous photo of men in single file with signs that said "I *am* a Man" while National Guardsmen stood nearby with fixed bayonets.

On Saturday, March 30, I met at the Peabody with Wurf, the AFSCME president, and P. J. Ciampa, an AFSCME organizer; and Bill Lucy and Baxton Bryant and others. I arrived at 10:00 a.m., and I had a session with Bryant there. I think that was the date on which Bryant made his appeal on behalf of the Tennessee Council on Human Relations to the U.S. Commission to hold a hearing in Memphis on the police brutality, and sent a telegram.

While there I met with the Community Relations Service people and our staff and Frank Miles. Frank was a labor negotiator and long time associate of Mayor Loeb. He came in and told us where things were. He was, by this time, in the negotiations. We wanted to be informed, and we wanted Frank to know everything we knew. We spent several hours with him. I also spoke with the attorney at the Justice Department's Civil Rights Division.

The incident of Larry Payne, the sixteen-year-old boy shot dead by police, was very much on our minds by then. The U. S. Commission on Civil Rights got involved in that immediately. I didn't have too much to do with it myself other than going to the scene. We were directed by Wilmore, our national director, "Go down there, find the people, and talk to them." Mrs. Miller and Bobby Doctor contacted Mrs. Payne, the dead boy's mother, and other members of the family. We went to the housing project, and had them come to our office. We took statements from them. I said, "Is this where Larry Payne lived and where did it happen?" I did this in broad daylight, moving as easy and relaxed as I could. But we got to the point at which we knew there were hostilities—and that it made more sense to let a black person do certain things instead of a white one. We sent the statements to the FBI.

That afternoon, still on Saturday, I was at the Minimum Salary Building where an informal session was being held. The spontaneity illustrated how we worked. Usually, when a meeting was over, we'd say, "We'll meet again at four o'clock tomorrow afternoon." On this day no meeting had been called. People were drifting in and out of the Minimum Salary Building. There were a handful of people. I asked whoever was there, "Where is so-and-so? What's happening and what's next?" Malcolm Blackburn was there, Billy Kyles, probably Bobby Doctor. Jim Bevel, Southern Christian Leadership Conference organizer and close associate of Dr. King's, appeared. I don't think he had been in before. Dr. Ralph Jackson, and probably Jesse Epps were there. Bill Lucy was there. Malcolm Blackburn was usually around; his office was on the same floor. The few individuals attending were well known to one another, except I had never met Jim Bevel.

We relaxed a little bit. Ralph Jackson brought a bottle into the room; he said a constituent, a friend, had brought it over from Arkansas. As I recall the Memphis liquor stores were ordered closed during this time. He placed it on the table and two or three people helped themselves and were properly grateful for it. The boycott of the newspapers was on, so you weren't supposed to be buying the papers. But we had a copy of the Sunday paper and there was this full-color ad for firearms. It gave a phone number you could call to obtain a gun. Someone was taking calls twenty-four hours a day. We talked about that and wondered whether a caller whose voice might be recognized as black would be allowed to purchase a gun. None of us tried, at least not then and there.

We met again later that night and others from SCLC came in. That might have been the night Jesse Jackson came in. They talked about where they would stay. Would they stay at Linden Lodge or would they stay at the Lorraine? Dr. King always stayed at the Lorraine, they said, so they would be at the Lorraine.

The next week a meeting was held to discuss holding another march, again to be led by Dr. King. He was bound and determined to carry out a peaceful march. Many of his closest associates were skeptical. They saw no reason why a second attempt would succeed any more than the first. It was a night meeting held at the sanitation worker's suite at the Lorraine. Wurf was there along with Bayard Rustin, a close associate of Dr. King's. We were joined by a Justice Department attorney named Owen; he had been with the Civil Rights Division, Justice Department, for a number of years and had come to Memphis as the representative of the U.S. Attorney General, Ramsey Clark. Owen was observing the conduct of all the law enforcement agencies. He was using offices in the federal building, in the district attorney's office, Tom Robinson's office. There were the two Community Relation Division men from the Justice Department, Ozelle Sutton and Fred Miller. Miller was a big, burly, red-faced white man from Georgia who blended into the scenery very well in Mississippi and Alabama and Georgia and Tennessee. We were all trying to plan a march, and to make sure it was nonviolent.

We talked about protection on the new march. Methods discussed included federalizing the National Guard and bringing in a considerable number of U.S. marshals.

The announcement for the march came sometime that week. The date was set for April 8. Immediately, the city asked federal Judge Bailey Brown to enjoin the march. One could hardly blame the city after what had happened. Judge Bailey Brown issued a temporary restraining order, and the SCLC— acting just as fast as the city had—hired local attorney Lucius Burch to fight the city's effort. A court date was set for April 5 to hear the injunction before Brown's court. Burch by then had cemented his reputation as a defense lawyer. He was also one of the city's best-known political activists, having led the fight to remove Boss Crump from power. People serious about winning a case or defeating a demigod wanted Burch on their side.

With the failure of my previous two meetings to bring about a solution to the strike, I had decided to enlist the help of the city's two newspaper editors. I had telephoned Frank Ahlgren of the *Commercial Appeal* and Charlie Schneider of the *Memphis Press-Scimitar*. I was on a first-name basis with both of these men. I had known Schneider since 1962 when he came to Memphis. I'd known Ahlgren all the way back to 1950, since my earliest days as a newspaperman. I said, "I want to come see you; what time tomorrow can I see you?" They each proposed a time. In our meetings, I told each of them I wanted a list of about twenty-five or thirty people, members of the white power structure, nothing but the people at the top, in their judgment. Charlie said, "You know as well as I do who these people are." I told him I wasn't in as close touch with Memphis as I was when I was on the paper. "I want your list. Take some time and think about it. You can mail it to me or I'll come back and get it." I said the same thing to Frank Ahlgren. I told each that I was seeing the other. I said, "It doesn't make any difference if your list duplicates the other's."

Of course there were numerous duplications on the two lists. (See Appendix A.) But using the lists, I drafted a letter (See Appendix B) very carefully inviting each of those named to any of three *ad hoc* meetings on how to gain a fair settlement for the striking workers. I suggested we might achieve progress with "plain honest talk."

I reasoned that we wanted no more than twenty people in such a meeting; this was a maximum or optimum number for discussion. Whenever you're inviting so many people, it takes a mathematician to figure out the slim probabilities that everyone would choose to attend the same meeting. With three meetings, surely somebody would choose to attend all three, and just as certainly some people would prefer attending just one.

I said in these letters, "I've gotten your name from a friend of yours and if you want to know who suggested that I invite you, I'll be glad to tell you." I wanted to be backed up by prestige or the force of the editors so that if somebody got on the phone and said, "John, what do you want me to come to this meeting for?" I would be able to say, "Well, Frank Ahlgren and Charlie Schneider think you ought to be there." Then I made a list of the city's black leaders and invited them, also by letter. I had not invited as many of them as I had whites. In my mind it wasn't too important to have equal numbers; a fair representation was what I was after. I wanted to be sure the whites got a clear impression that there were black leaders whom they didn't know and should know. It was primarily the white business community I was aiming at, so they would know about the importance of this issue. I still had the thought that these people would be persuaded to bring pressure not only on the mayor but on the city council, if need be.

I allowed people to choose which one or more of the three meetings they would come to. It was important to me to say in the letter to the whites and the blacks that we were holding these meetings at a black place, and we were holding them at a white or a neutral place. This provided a choice of places and times. The first was scheduled for Friday, April 5 at the YWCA on Monroe. The next was to be held that afternoon at the Tri-State Bank. The third was scheduled for Saturday morning, April 6, back at the YWCA. On the afternoon of April 3, I carried the letters to the Desoto Station post office. I knew it was important that the letters go out right away. I was running late and I sent them Special Delivery, thinking they'd be delivered that same day.

I sometimes wonder how things might have turned out differently had I moved more quickly.

On the evening of April 3, I took my son John to hear Dr. King speak at Mason Temple. The church was packed; we sat in the gallery. The subject, of course, was the injustice being suffered by the city's sanitation workers. It was powerful. The audience listened and wept.

Well, I don't know what will happen now. We've got some difficult days ahead. But it doesn't matter with me now. Because I've been to the mountaintop. And I don't mind. Like anybody, I would like to live a long life. Longevity has its place. But I'm not concerned about that now. I just want to do God's will. And He's allowed me to go up to the mountain. And I've looked over. And I've seen the promised land. I may not get there with you. But I want you to know tonight, that we, as a people, will get to the promised land. And I'm happy, tonight. I'm not worried about anything. I'm not fearing any man. Mine eyes have seen the glory of the coming of the Lord.

King hadn't been well; he'd considered not speaking on this rainy night. When he finished, he had to be helped to his seat. It would be his last speech.

On the morning of April 4, we walked to the federal courthouse. I saw Burch as he was going to court. Here was this tall man, flanked by about three of his junior attorneys. I have a vivid memory of Charles Newman and Mike Cody—perhaps along with David Caywood—three young lawyers toting law books and heading up the street with Lucius, His Majesty. Carrying books was beneath Lucius's dignity. I suppose he carried a fountain pen. They strode off to go to court, to do battle for the sanitation workers.

Burch and attorney Lou Lucas called on me as one of the witnesses. They asked what I thought would happen if the march were prevented. I told the court that it would be bad if the right to march were denied. I said that the black people thought generally that the courts belonged to the white man, and that the whites just went through motions.

Later that afternoon a meeting was held in my office. This was a subcommittee of our Tennessee Advisory Committee. We invited the Memphis members: Jim Blackburn, Charles Poole, Dan Powell, Russell Sugarmon, and Billy Kyles. Henry Forgy from Jackson had come in. We made a plan of action to hold a closed meeting on the allegations of police brutality. We left the meeting at about 5:30. I took Henry Forgy to my house. He and I were sitting in my kitchen when the telephone rang. It was a friend calling to tell us that Dr. King had been shot. "Did you hear the news on the radio?" I said, no, I hadn't. Without ever hearing anything on the air, Henry and I got in the car and headed for the John Gaston Hospital.

I picked John Gaston because I thought this would be a repeat of the James Meredith shooting in 1966; Meredith had been shot on Highway 51 near Hernando about the same time of day and he was taken to John Gaston hospital. I supposed this would also be done with Dr. King. But at the John Gaston there was no action. We knew then it had to be St. Joseph's.

We saw the people outside. Mostly blacks, not in large numbers. There were police cars parked all around. People were standing at the main entrance. I went inside and headed toward the emergency room. Police were inside the corridors. I saw others weeping. They were angry and already there were some rumors about fires set in retaliation.

I didn't know whether Dr. King was alive or dead. I didn't learn much from the first two or three people I asked. One was an assistant administrator who didn't know what was happening. Nor did the switchboard operator. You couldn't expect them to, not really. I kept pushing my way in.

At the emergency room, I found David Caywood. It seemed like Caywood was everywhere. There we saw Andy Young and others I can't recall. Hosea Williams may have been there. Big Jim Orange might have. Ben Hooks, I saw him. A few people were standing in the corridor. It was a long corridor with several sets of doors. Not many people would barge through those, even without guards. People are usually slow to barge in through a long succession of closed doors. There wasn't much you could say.

I was there only about fifteen minutes. You rush in and you know that anything that you can honestly do to calm people you will do. And so I sought some word. No announcement had been made. Caywood said, "He's still alive." I rushed back up to the front to say to a police officer. "Tell these people he's alive." I don't know whether the police officer did that. It may have been untrue. Then I went back toward the emergency room. There I saw Young and the SCLC people. They were in tears and it was real awful.

There were other emergencies. We saw a man brought out on a stretcher, covered. I think he was a white man.

Shortly afterward, I met Gerry Fanion and Jim Lawson and Ben Hooks. Gerry drove Henry and me, along with Jim and Ben. Our first stop was WREC-TV. Then we drove to WHBQ-TV, and finally to WMC-TV, in that order. The five of us made this round. I felt that as whites, Henry and I were there to observe and protect. It didn't matter that it was Judge Hooks, and Gerry Fanion, and Rev. Jim Lawson—they were just three black men driving around after curfew. And so we wanted to be along. There was no conversation about this.

We were not stopped. We asked for a police escort and the police arrived at WHBQ-TV about the time we did. They stayed with us to WMC-TV. Henry was getting concerned about not having talked with his wife. Gerry dropped Henry and me off at my house. I picked up my car and Henry took his, which he'd left there. The police had followed Gerry from WHBQ to WMCT and I think as far as my house. We lost them on Central and Willett.

Looking back I realize that by the time Hooks and Lawson went on the air at WREC-TV, the public already knew King was dead, as did we. I don't know how we knew. I must have known he was dead when I left the hospital, though I didn't say anything publicly about it at that point.

After I dropped off Henry, I drove to the police station. I stood mostly in the corridor; then I was in the office of first one assistant chief and then another. I watched as suspects of recent crimes were brought in. They were photographed, frisked, and made to surrender their personal possessions. I saw a good deal of blood. I didn't hear any abusive language.

I stayed for Director Holloman's 12:30 a.m. press conference. Holloman kept the press waiting. He came into the conference room red-eyed and tired, but affable, carrying some papers in front of him. Of course, what they wanted to know was all about Dr. King's assassin—his apprehension and identification. Holloman was able to tell them that they had the gun or a gun, which might have been the gun and it was such-and-such a weapon and so on. There were a lot of newsmen there. The *Los Angeles Times* had two reporters there that night, Nelson and Crisp. The *Washington Post* had someone there as well.

Almost everything changed. It didn't change the fact that the strikers still would want their union, of course. Sadly, it did not seem to change the city's wanting them to go back to work without a union. So the next day I went ahead with the plan to hold three meetings on April 5 and 6. The Friday morning following the assassination we had a reasonably good turnout, all things considered: about twelve to fifteen people. We met in the library room on the second floor of the YWCA, where the Memphis Committee on Community Relations so often met.

Naturally, I expected the blacks I had invited would not show. Yet two actually did attend: Ozelle Sutton, with the Community Relations Service, Department of Justice, and Bill Lucy, AFSCME organizer. Neither one was a Memphian, but both were well equipped to talk to the whites who were there. Sutton was a Southerner from Little Rock, and a former newspaperman. He had been trying to learn about Memphis; he had been on the scene a good deal. I had called Lucy that morning: "Bill, I need you to come." He came and he did a splendid job of demonstrating to a group of white men that here was an intelligent, aggressive, sophisticated, and reasonably objective black man arguing and fighting the case for the sanitation workers.

The meeting lasted about two hours. We felt as if we might have made some progress toward settling the strike, or at least getting the conversation moving in the right direction. Otherwise, we achieved no concrete results.

I went ahead with the Friday afternoon meeting at the Tri-State Bank, not expecting many people. One showed up. This was Sam Britt, the vice president for personnel at First National Bank. He was substituting for Allen Morgan, who was out of the city. Sam and I sat and talked for about thirty minutes or so. Since nobody else showed up, that was it. The next day, April 6, I saw no reason to wait on anybody; I could see there wasn't going to be anyone. By now, of course, other matters loomed.

I've often thought about what might have happened had these meetings been held a week earlier, had I not waited until near the end of March to call the newspaper editors and send out the invitations. So many events came close to ending the strike and who knows what another push or two might have done to end the stalemate before the catastrophe at the Lorraine Hotel ended Dr. King's life.

Martin Luther King was an American prophet. Had he lived on, had he overseen a successful march culminating in the end of the strike, he might have gone on and succeeded with his Poor People's Campaign. Who knows how that might have changed the American landscape? But it was not to be. The stars weren't in line and the angels weren't with us.

By now people realized that the peaceful march King and others had worked so hard for *had* to be held. The so-called Memorial March was now scheduled for Monday. So on April 6 there were two meetings, one around noon and the other in late afternoon, to go over the details of the march. Bayard Rustin was there. Rustin was close to Dr. King and had organized the 1963 March on Washington. City officials were there: Holloman, Armour, and many others. The National Guard was also represented. In a few isolated spots, it seemed there was no great resentment among blacks regarding the presence of the police at the many demonstrations. Men would jive at the police occasionally, or make remarks among themselves. "Gosh, why does it take so many officers to police this little old demonstration?" Mostly what I was hearing were these very natural jives. We would hear occasionally from policemen themselves that they were tired of working all this overtime. "I sure haven't had much rest."

On the next night, Sunday, I walked with Rustin along the march route, block by block and step by step. There must have been a dozen of us standing in the middle of Hernando near the Minimum Salary Building about one o'clock in the morning, when we were stopped by the National Guard. Up rolled this six-by-six and a jeep. We had a police captain or assistant chief along with us to tell them it was all right for us to be there.

The march went off with scarcely a hitch. Tens of thousands joined in. While cities such as Washington, D.C., Louisville, Chicago, and Baltimore were rioting in the wake of the assassination, that did not happen here.

During the march, I stood at the corner of Vance and Hernando talking with a couple of city policemen who were parked there. They were both black policemen, and the marchers had finally gone by and I was back on the tag end with Jerry Fanion. He and I and the police talked very pleasantly. They asked us what we knew. Fanion had his citizens band radio, and spent two or three minutes with them there. I was in and out of the police station a number of nights afterward just to see what went on.

The assassination of Martin Luther King shocked the nation into recognizing what the sanitation workers had been up against. It finally proved instrumental in settling the strike. President Lyndon Johnson sent down the Under Secretary of Labor James Reynolds with orders not to come home until the strike was settled. Ten days later, the strike was formally ended when the City Council approved a memorandum of agreement that recognized the workers' union with the dues collecting ("check-off") powers intact. It also awarded them a pay raise.[18]

I believe we achieved a lot during the civil rights era, but not as much as we thought we would. We were naively hopeful about what we thought we could do, which was to break down racial lines and open up opportunities. Much of that has occurred, but not as much as we expected. We weren't exactly disappointed, but we shifted more from enthusiasm to understanding. We've had a great deal of change. We have a more culturally integrated society today. I notice it when I go out to lunch, here and there. I take it for granted we're going to see blacks in most any restaurant I go—though we still have a long way to go before we can call our society fully integrated.

What I didn't anticipate was a loss of the fraternal feeling that prevailed during the early movement. We expected that the warmth, maybe some gratitude, would endure, perhaps increase. It didn't. Perhaps that's just as well. The success depended on blacks doing their own thing. That's what we wanted them to do, and they did, in time.

Chapter Twenty-One

Personal Matters

In 1969, I decided to quit my job at the U.S. Commission on Civil Rights. The price we paid for settling the sanitation strike had been too high. With King's assassination, the city reeled under the strain of national and international condemnation. Businesses pulled out, and tourism declined. Memphis lost its reputation as a friendly town.

In the meantime, tension between the traditional civil rights workers and those pushing for black empowerment had grown. The black leaders were beginning to say to us white folks: "We don't need you. We don't want to be leaning on you."

Too, it became clear I would not be awarded a top post in the Civil Rights Commission. That year I stepped away from the public life. My activism became more personal.

My son John disliked ROTC, as probably 90 percent of boys did. This was during the Vietnam War. Boys everywhere were looking for ways not to go to Vietnam. John considered going to Canada. As a senior at Central High School, he decided to assert he was a conscientious objector and defer from taking ROTC. But on account of his boycotting ROTC, the school refused to award John his high school diploma. This was a mean and funny thing. The Memphis Board of Education was trying to get physical education on the cheap with ROTC. They didn't want to go to the expense and trouble of building gymnasiums and hiring phys ed teachers. Instead they told the kids to put on uniforms and march around, and call that phys ed. (Back in the Thirties in the midst of the Depression we were all delighted to have Uncle Sam provide our clothing. I don't know that we were allowed to wear our uniforms five days a week, but it was an economic consideration with us. In 1932 and 1933, when I was at Central, every boy in the school took at least two years in ROTC. I think you could be exempt as a senior if you wanted to.)

We never tried to work it out with the School Board. That would have been a waste of time. I knew that. After all, I had covered the school board as a reporter. I knew the members. We already had a run-in with them in the case of my daughter, Marty. Instead we took it to the courts.

In 1969, the ACLU took up our case, *ACLU v. the Memphis Board of Education*. Our case was a federal case, a First Amendment case, a civil rights issue. David Caywood, a member of Lucius Burch's firm, represented the ACLU. David would not have accepted it if he had considered his friendship with me as any factor at all. Actually, he was an acquaintance, somebody I might have had a meal or two with. I was friends with Lucius Burch and that was as close as we were. In any event, it was tried in Judge Bailey Brown's U.S. District court. Brown and I had attended high school together, but we hardly knew each other; I could remember Mary Ann and I being guests one time in his apartment in Kimbrough Towers.

We won. But the school board took it on appeal in Cincinnati at the Federal Court of Appeals, Sixth Circuit. The school board is always trying to spend public money trying to have things their way. They were spending public money and I was spending private. Ramsey Clark was now one of the lawyers on the Court of Appeals. He had been Lyndon Johnson's attorney general, and is still remembered as a staunch defender of civil liberties and civil rights. He wrote the appeal in our case. We won. That was it. The school board probably knew it was stupid of them to try to take it on to the U.S. Supreme Court. The decision changed the school policies toward mandatory ROTC. I've always taken pleasure in this. We went on a belief. John didn't believe in killing, didn't believe in shooting people.

In 1974, following his graduation from Rhodes College, John was elected to the Tennessee Legislature. It was a proud day when the ballots were counted, showing John the winner. He represented our district in Nashville for the next eight years.

In 1969, I decided to become a college professor. I returned to college, to Southwestern and completed the degree I'd so ignominiously failed to get some thirty years earlier. In 1970, I was admitted into Vanderbilt to pursue a master's degree in political science. A boyhood friend, Leiper Freeman of Murfreesboro, served on the Vanderbilt faculty. It was due to him, I believe, that I owe my admittance; I have no evidence to support my belief, unless it is that I got no offer from the other university to which I applied. (I am bound to record that I was something of a fathead about my interview at the other graduate school. My interviewer, a gruff man somewhat older than I, ended the meeting by saying, "Well, I think I've heard enough." I, fatuously, decided that meant I had passed muster. It was the last I ever heard from him.)

During this time my daughter Marty, then twenty, was attending Barnard College in New York City. Son John was studying at Rhodes College in Memphis. Mary Ann was also at Rhodes, overseeing the work part of the work/study programs of several students. Mary Ann liked to say with pride that she was the only working member of the family. I think we all were proud of her. I did have to struggle to make the grades but finally earned an M.A. in political science. My thesis was on law enforcement administration. It was a timely topic, though not so interesting in retrospect.

I wrote letters to four colleges and universities seeking a faculty position. Three offered me a job, all in Memphis. I chose Shelby State Community College near downtown Memphis, which was just opening up.

Shelby State was brand new. I was on the first faculty there. I taught political science, journalism, and U.S. history.

The year was 1972. We had no buildings of our own, so we occupied an older part of the Veterans Administration hospital built during World War II. That worked well for several years, until the new campus was built. My students were Memphis and Shelby County young people.

The political science courses I taught were, of course, introductory or elementary. I taught U.S. government, state and local government, and a comparative politics course. I also taught U.S. history. I am quite proud of getting my students to believe in themselves as political activists. The first assignment I gave them was to get themselves registered to vote. For many, this was an exciting activity, giving them pride and confidence. For some, the visit to the government offices was a first experience; they had never set foot in such places, had to learn where they were, realize that the officials behind the counters were just like themselves. The students came back to class smiling and confident.

I had some good students. The pre-nursing and nursing students were exceptionally good. The earlier and later the class was scheduled in the day, the better the students. If they had to get up and come to school early, they wanted to learn. Or if they wanted to attend after a hard day's work, they might fall asleep in class but their intentions were good. Students dreaded afternoon classes. I used to sleep in afternoon classes myself.

I was sixty-four and had taught more than ten years in the Tennessee system, all at Shelby State. In 1983 I gave up teaching. With time on my hands, I began reflecting back on my war years. It was something I rarely spoke of. I certainly didn't consider myself a war hero. I had been paying dues to the 303rd bomber group. Back in 1945 and 1946, I joined the American Legion and the VFW, but I was out of them in a year or two. It wasn't my dish. A friend told me about the Air Forces Escape and Evasion Society in the late 1980s.

Organized in the 1960s, AFEES's purpose is to encourage those like me who were aided by resistance organizations to continue friendships with those who helped them. The first meeting I attended, I went alone to San Antonio; then I went to Pittsburgh. I brought the organization to Memphis in 1990 during the Memphis in May Festival.

On that occasion, Mary Ann and I brought Genevieve Noufflard and Jeannette Penne, two women most important to my successful escape from occupied France, to Memphis as the conference's honored attendees. They stayed at our home. That was the beginning of the renewal of the friendship with Jeannette; along with Genevieve, who had been close, visiting off and on with us since 1945 when she was a guest in my mother's house on Faxon Avenue. We all had a good time.

I have led several civic efforts. One was to create the Mid-Memphis Political Forum, with help from Anne Shafer and Tandy Gilliland. It's now known as the Public Issues Forum. Mary Ann and I created a fine list of potential members, and we held monthly breakfasts at the Admiral Benbow Motel on Union and Bellevue. Jim Gilliland was our first speaker. We had good turnouts, about twenty or thirty folks. Some were young, some old; all were mostly liberal sorts. I thought of issues, got the speakers, put out the newsletter. I enjoyed it and it was worthwhile. Those who attended remember it gratefully.

In 1985, along with Charles Cooley, Esther West, and Charles Newman, I co-formed the Wolf River Conservancy, a nonprofit group that has done well protecting one of Memphis's greatest natural resources. I have enjoyed the many hours floating down the Wolf River, and the fellowship with those like-minded outdoorsmen and women.

Around the same time, Mary Ann took responsibility for the church supper on Wednesday nights at St. John's Methodist Church. People today remember her as a tireless worker. Someone said without Mary Ann, they wouldn't have been able to feed all those people.

In 1990 my daughter Marty was teaching and painting. My son John left an investment firm and struck out on his own, investing in banks and opening a partnership. He moved to Nashville, married Angela Murphy, and had two children.

Epilogue

As my father related in his wartime reminiscences, he had told her his name. That's how, after the war was over, Genevieve tracked him down. Genevieve Noufflard was the young French woman, of Jewish parentage, who had taken the risk of hosting my father on afternoon walks while he was underground in Paris. She visited our family several times when she came to the United States touring as a concert flutist and, in the 1970s, as an interpreter for the composer of a new Catholic hymnal.

Upon his retirement – and better able to look at his WWII experience from a distance – my father joined the Air Forces Escape and Evasion Society. He was subsequently asked, by various organizations, to tell his World War II escape story. Thus, encouraged by many, he began to write this memoir, and decided to return to France to find and thank the people who aided in his escape. He made three trips. In 1977, he found that M. le Comte and Mme. la Comtesse de Keranflec had died and their chateau had passed to their grand-nephew, Vicomte Bertrand de Saint Pierre. He also received word of Jeannette Gueguec Pennes, the young woman who had given him her father's clothes moments after his plane was shot down. He retraced his steps from the village of Paule along the Brest Canal to the chateau and the Plaintel train station.

He returned to France again in 1992 to join a celebration commemorating the courage, daring, and generosity of the farmers, housewives, and merchants of Brittany. On this trip he found Catherine Janot and the descendants of his Parisian protectors, the Tinel family, whose son Jacques had been apprehended and killed by the Germans. In 1994, my father returned to Paris where, at the Tinel family home, he was awarded the Medal of St. Cloud.

Here in Memphis, my father persuaded the board and director of the Dixon Gallery to become the first American museum to mount a large exhibit of artwork by the Impressionist painters Andre and Berthe Noufflard, Genevieve's parents. In 1988, my father hosted Genevieve and her sister, Henriette, when they came to view the exhibit. The Noufflards' art exhibit then toured to six other distinguished American art museums, demonstrating one small, enduring bond between France and the United States as the result of one soldier's WWII experience.

John Wilson Spence died on March 11, 2008, and his wife, Mary Ann, on January 18, 2015. They are both buried at Elmwood Cemetery with John's parents.

Marty Spence (with Lisa Jo Sagolla)
August 2017

Notes

1. (page vi) Editor's Note: Among John Spence's papers, at the University of Memphis Libraries/Special Collections, there are some photographs taken during his father's time in the Philippines.

2. (page 12) Years later, during the Great Depression, the Mooney School lost its luster and the property became a rooming house.

3. (page 14) A tale is told that the girls in the school roller-skated in the huge upper hall of the antebellum mansion. Decades later, when I took my wife and children to visit, the school had become a museum.

4. (page 14) Although the term has fallen into disuse, a *normal school* is a teacher-training college. West Tennessee State Normal School is now the University of Memphis.

5. (page 15) Hammond was son of Seymour A. Mynders, the first president of the college. The administration building, Mynders Hall, at the University of Memphis, was named for him.

6. (page 17) George M. Darrow had married well: Memphis belle Tempe (or Tempie) Swope had inherited a large Mississippi cotton plantation, and Mr. Darrow was a good steward. So good that in 1884 the Darrows bought Murfreesboro's Oaklands mansion at auction from the last of the Maney family and restored it to glory. Soon they grew tired of living "in the country" and

bought a lot at the corner of East Main Street and Highland Avenue, which is where they lived when I knew them.

7. (page 19) Murfreesboroans always said "Maney's Avenue." Since the street ran straight into the Maney ancestral home, called Oaklands Mansion now, this habit may have dated from a time before there were many street names in Murfreesboro.

8. (page 24) The city of Memphis began converting gaslights as early as 1884, but it took some time to convert a city of more than one hundred thousand.

9. (page 25) Editor's Note: "Expecting a sturdy climber and bold adventurer with a particularly masculine writing style, Thomas Bailey Aldrich, her Boston editor at Houghton & Mifflin, was astonished to meet a petite woman in a 'rolling chair'," reported Eleanor B. Spence in her biographical thesis, *Collected Reminiscences of Mary Noailles Murfree*, 1928, George Peabody College for Teachers. Physically disabled by a childhood illness, Mary Noailles Murfree (1850-1922) is considered by many to be Appalachia's first significant female writer and her work a necessity for the study of Appalachian literature. The author of 25 books, she was an important member of the post-Civil War American local-color movement and has been favorably compared to Bret Harte and Sarah Orne Jewett.

10. (page 27) These included Augusta Young, Ethel Brown, later Mrs. Grider Wiggs, and Alice Brignardello. Mother liked all of them and they were delighted with her.

11. (page 27) An Irish mail is a velocipede: four wheels with leather tires, a wooden seat, and a handle the rider moves up and back, which propels it

forward, much like a railroad handcar. They were very popular in the early 1900s. The origin of the name is unclear.

12. (page 37) Shocking as it may be to contemporary readers, most children were forced to switch well into the 1960s. The practice has been largely abandoned in the United States.

13. (page 45) Sewanee Military Academy originated as the Sewanee Grammar School for Boys in 1861, and was a preparatory department of the University of the South. In 1908 it became the Sewanee Military Academy, although I'm not sure that the affiliation with the university remained.

14. (page 62) This was the Aviation Cadet Pilot Training Program, created by the U.S. Army.

15. (page 150) Ruth Sulzberger later divorced him. Her nephew, Arthur O. Sulzberger, became the *New York Times* chairman in 1992 and CEO in 2011.

16. (page 185) Russell Sugarmon was later a General Sessions Court judge.

17. (page 185) Jesse Turner, a wonderful man, came up from Mississippi after World War II service. He was an accountant. He ran the Tri-State Bank for its owners, the Maceo Walker family and heirs of Robert W. Church.

18. (page 220) Editor's Note: Almost 50 years later (as reported in a July 26, 2017, *New York Times* article), the city of Memphis decided to award grants of $50,000 each to the 14 surviving strikers in an attempt to rectify the inequity that spurred the black sanitation workers strike of 1968.

Acknowledgments

The posthumous editing of a deceased author's memoir presents unusual problems. In this instance, the author's story had to be gleaned mostly from a box of assorted typescripts in which the author made repeated attempts to cover portions of his life from different angles and in different time periods. These materials along with interviews, assorted newspaper clippings, and other materials, provide a painting of the author's life. For their generous help, I'm grateful to the author's children, Marty Spence and John Spence, III. Marty offered a collection of family records, including photographs and newspaper clippings. John, whom I've known for many years, provided the inspiration for completing the project. Most of all, I owe my thanks to the Spence family for entrusting me with the project.

In the early 1950s John met my father, George Grider, another decorated war veteran. They joined a small group of progressives pushing for political reform. Politics and the mutual love of the outdoors cast Spence and Grider into a lifelong friendship. In 1964 Grider was elected to Congress, and opened a Memphis office of the U.S. Commission on Civil Rights. Spence happily accepted Grider's offer of a job on the staff, putting to use his political savvy and contacts to help heal the racially torn community.

As a young man, I first got to know John Spence when he and my father would invite me on duck hunts. Over the years we developed a lasting friendship. In 1998 following my father's death, John persuaded my wife and me to move to Memphis from our home in San Diego. In 2001 we sat down with a tape recorder and began assembling the events of his life. The limited output from the interviews, I considered insufficient for a manuscript.

Fortunately when John died in 2008, Marty presented me with a box of typescripts, material he'd been working on alone. At Marty's and John Jr's request, I began compiling the material. Nearly every word in this book is his. Exceptions consist of a few unrecorded but often-mentioned facts heard during our long walks around the neighborhood. A few small sections were composed to give the work continuity.

The book would not have reached the level of readability it deserves had it not been for the editors who assisted in the manuscript's production. Jamie Chavez, a freelance editor and my chief assistant, undertook the grueling task of editing every word and paragraph, making the story read as smoothly as if it were being told over a campfire. Jamie, a long-time resident of Murfreesboro, Tennessee, also provided valuable historical footnotes. Laura Helper-Ferris of Helper-Ferris Editorial Agency helped get the project underway during the difficult early stages by identifying key passages and suggesting various structures.

Stored archives pertaining to John's family were generously provided by Ed Frank, curator of the Department of Preservation and Special Collections of the University of Memphis McWherter Library. Transcripts of John Spence's interviews from the Memphis Search for Meaning Committee in June 1968 add incalculable value. David Yellin and Bill Thomas of the Memphis Search for Meaning Committee undertook the exhaustive interviews with John concerning those final days of the sanitation workers strike.

Thanks to Mike Kerr of *The Commercial Appeal* for giving permission to republish the author's articles appearing in the now defunct *Memphis Press-Scimitar*, both owned by the E. W. Scripps Company.

For providing interviews from 2002 with the author on his war experience, I'm grateful to the University of Tennessee, College of Arts & Sciences, Center for the Study of War and Society, Ms. Cynthia Tinker, project coordinator. The interviews were conducted by Dr. Kurt Piehler and Nashwa Van Houts.

A special thanks to the Liberty Foundation for sending a B-17 bomber to the Olive Branch Airport, Mississippi, in 2012. Thanks to docent Jason Robinson for allowing me an inside look at the four-engine "Flying Fortress" in which John and his fellow crewmembers entrusted their lives, but from which not everyone returned home safely.

A special thanks to Sue Vance, member of the Eutaw, Alabama, Chamber of Commerce. Ms. Vance led John's daughter Marty and me on a tour of Eutaw, pointing out the landmarks that survive the seventy years since the time of John's story, including Mary Wheeler's tombstone.

Lastly, many thanks to John Pritchard, Kirk Loggins, and Bryan Curtis for leading me to Jamie Chavez. With added appreciation for the final editorial assistance of Lisa Jo Sagolla.

George W. Grider, Jr.

Appendix A:
Recipients of the Special Delivery Invitation

List of white establishment leaders who received the invitation to private "honest talk" meetings mailed Special Delivery, 4/3/68. (Based on list provided by Mr. Frank Ahlgren, Editor, *Commercial Appeal*.)

Walter Armstrong, Attorney, Commerce Title Building
Julian Bondurant, Wells Fargo Armored Service Corp.
Bayard Boyle, Boyle Investment Co.
Carl Carson, Carl Carson Co.
Sam Cooper, President, HumKo. (Jack Kopald, sec-treas., accepted.)
Ray Cummins, President, Goldsmith's
Donald Drinkard, William R. Moore, Inc.
Thomas Faires, President, Chamber of Commerce
Bert Ferguson, President, WDIA
Porter Grace, President, Union Planters National Bank
B. W. Hannock Jr., President, Lowenstein's
George Houston, Mid-South Title Co. Inc., Commerce Title Building
C. C. Humphreys, President, Memphis State University
Julius Lewis, President, Julius Lewis
Roy Marr, President, Leader Federal
James H. McCune, Plant Manager, Firestone Tire & Rubber Co.
Lewis McKee, President, National Bank of Commerce
LeRoy Montgomery, President, Real Estate Board
Allen Morgan, President, First National Bank
Philip Perel, President, Perel & Lowenstein
Abe Plough, President, Plough Inc.
Murray Reiter, Chairman, National Commission of Christians and Jews
John Rezba, General Manager, Kimberly-Clark
Pat Thayer, Thayer Construction Co.
J. L. Williams, Personnel Manager, International Harvester (*substituted for J. W. Wegener, mgr.*)
Kemmons Wilson, President, Holiday Inn of America, Inc.

List of black establishment leaders invited to private "honest talk" meetings. List provided by Frank Ahlgren. **NOTE:** No existing copy of letter sent members of this list found. They may have been personally contacted.

Ezekiel Bell, pastor, Parkway Gardens Presbyterian Church
Malcolm Blackburn, pastor, Clayborn AME Temple
Cornelia Crenshaw, housing project manager and community activist
H. Ralph Jackson, pastor, AME Church
S. B. Kyles, pastor, Monumental Baptist Church
James M. Lawson, pastor, Centenary Methodist Church
Bill Lucy, labor union organizer
Harry Middlebrook, assistant pastor, Middle Baptist Church
Gilbert E. Patterson, bishop, Church of God In Christ
James Smith, pastor, Union Grove Missionary Baptist Church
Maxine A. Smith, executive secretary, Memphis branch of NAACP
Henry L. Starks, pastor, St. James AME Church
Jesse H. Turner Sr., director, Memphis branch of NAACP

Appendix B:
"Plain Honest Talk"

Invitation to attend a series of three private "plain honest talk" meetings, on April 5 and 6, 1968, between "white power structure" and "black power stucture." Mailed April 3, 1968, Special Delivery, to white establishment leaders (see addresses below). The letter to the "black power structure" has been lost.

U.S. Commission of Civil Rights
Mid-South Field Office
Memphis, Tennessee 38104

April 3, 1968

Dear Mr.
Many good Memphians are working very hard in many ways to resolve the crisis brought upon this city by the continuation of the sanitation workers' strike.

We of the Southern Field Office of the U.S. Commission on Civil Rights have tried to do our duty by participating as observers—and where requested, as impartial advisers—to every identifiable group involved.

We have met with leaders of the American Federation of State, County and Municipal Employees. We have met with the "strategy committee" of Community on the Move for Equality. We have met with the Southern Christian Leadership Conference men now in the city. We have met with City Council members. We have attended—night after night and day after day, the church meetings and the Main Street marches.

We have met with the members of Local 1733 of the AFSCME. We have talked with the editors of our daily newspapers. We believe that we are fully informed as to negotiations between Mayor Loeb's four-member negotiating team and the five-member group for the strikers.

We are consulting, several times daily, with our Washington staff. We are trying to maintain liaison with the other Federal agencies which have men on the scene. We are assessing the possibilities of securing long-term aid from such Federal agencies as the Labor Department, Department of Housing and Urban Development, the Office of Economic Opportunity.

We are, we believe, leaving no stone unturned to bring men of good will and sense to a meeting of minds. Toward that end, we believe that there is absolutely no substitute for face-to-face discussions, privately and in a calm and friendly atmosphere.

The U.S. Commission on Civil Rights is attempting to arrange a series of three small, private meetings between "white power" and "black power." You are "white power," business power. Friends of yours—and on request we will tell you who—have urged us to invite you. The Negroes we are inviting are "black power" in the sense that they are leaders—responsible leaders—of the union, the Negro churches, Negro business and education.

This is an invitation to you to attend one of those three meetings. Places and times are listed below. It is our desire to see seated about 12 to 15 persons, white and black, who can talk for perhaps two hours about the issues dividing the city, both in the matter of the strike and the underlying discontent due to housing, health, welfare, employment, and education.

This letter goes to about 25 white business men. Ideally, about eight will attend each of the three meetings; about four or five Negro leaders will attend each session, and one or more members of our staff will be on hand for introductions, etc.

Is there something specific to be gained by your attending? We hope so.

First, we believe that concurrent with resumption of union-city negotiations of the strike issues—and in no way conflicting or duplicating—the white business leadership of Memphis can be informing itself and possibly coming to some conclusions re the strike and other issues.

Second, from talks with the Negro leaders you may learn how deep-seated are certain legitimate—and unmet—desires of Memphis Negroes in other areas—employment, etc. It seems very unlikely that this or any other large American city can forecast healthy growth unless we meet head-on the problems posed by the lack of plain honest talk between the groups you represent and the groups the Negro leaders represent.

We urge you: <u>Please attend</u> one of these meetings. Let us know by phone which you will come to. These are to be unpublicized meetings. So that you will not be tempted to do the natural thing and ask certain persons whom you think might be invited: "Have you been invited? Are you going?" and discover that you have inadvertently disclosed the meeting to someone not invited, we are attaching a list of the persons being invited. Do feel free to talk with any of these.

We are proposing three different meeting places:
YWCA library, 200 Monroe (third floor), 10:00 a.m. Friday [April 5, 1968].
Tri-State Bank directors room, 213 S. Main, 3:00 p.m. Friday
YWCA library, 200 Monroe, 10:00 a.m. Saturday. [April 6]

Our telephone numbers are 534-3139, 534-3130, 534-3877.

Forgive us for repeating ourselves, but once again we will ask: Please keep it confidential at least until the meetings have been held and you have decided whether, as a result, there is any need for further deliberation or action at another time and place.

Sincerely yours,
John W. Spence
Assistant Director

Appendix C:
John W. Spence's Newspaper Articles
1948-1965, Partial Listing*

The Covington Leader

4/29/48	Forbess, Moore Win Close Races In Democratic Primary
5/13/48	Ballard To Go On Trial Next Friday
5/13/48	Diamond Season Opening Tuesday At Athletic Field
5/13/48	Jaycees Give First Fish Fry of Year
5/13/48	Price Boom About To Bust Says Prof.
5/13/48	Ginn Wins National Scholarship Award
5/13/48	Editorial Page: One Way To Get Limit
5/13/48	Editorial Page: Cotton Is New Fabric
5/20/48	Baptists Making Church History In Memphis Session
5/20/48	Excited Fans See Brighton Win 9-7 Game With Owen
5/20/48	Fescue On Farms Here Living Up To Reputation Made In Kentucky
5/20/48	Acuff Sought For Night of June 15
5/20/48	Red Cross Offers Swimming Lessons
5/20/48	U.S. Hatchery Is Sending 3750 Fish
5/20/48	Alaska Calls Five On 3000-Mile Drive
5/20/48	Cockrill Returning To Shop On Highway
5/20/48	Brownsville Will Vote on Blue Law
5/20/48	Editorial Page: A Puff At Coals And Cause
5/27/48	V.F.W. Hangs Out 'No Vacancy' Sign
5/27/48	County Chalks Up Campaign Victory
5/27/48	Governor Will Get Highway Petition
5/27/48	Highway Assured, City Is Filing Condemnation Suits
5/27/48	Power Sale Nets City $46,000 In Last 12 Months
5/27/48	G.O.P. Lets Trade Act Live One Year
5/27/48	60 Girls Handle Publicity For National Donkey Baseball Chain
5/27/48	Shoaf Will Manage Browning Campaign
5/27/48	Brannan Truman's Cabinet Selection
5/27/48	Four Tipton Boys Are Joining Army
5/27/48	Vaughan to Plant More Milo Maize
5/27/48	Editorial Page: The Price May Be High

5/27/48	Editorial Page: To Boys And Their Parents
5/27/48	New Teams Given Rugged Reception
5/27/48	Paratrooper Lands In SCS Work Here
6/3/48	Flames Lick Gym At Munford High
6/3/48	Customer Given A Break in Covington
6/3/48	She Skipped Dance, Won Scholarship
6/3/48	Children Will Learn Easier Next Year: They'll Do It With Movies
6/3/48	Children Swarm Over Playground On Opening Day
6/3/48	Browning, McCord Decline Invitation
6/3/48	Editorial Page: Room For Improvement
6/3/48	Browning to Open Campaign Saturday
6/3/48	Editorial Page: We Tire of Fumbling and Bungling
6/10/48	Bored Softball Fans Get Break From Rule
6/10/48	Waters of Pond Close Over Two Peeler Children
6/10/48	School In Mason Unites Churches
6/10/48	Primary Board For Election is Named
6/10/48	Editorial Page: Don't Bar Ambition And Brains

The Chattanooga Times

1/4/49	Speakers Herald Good '49 Business
1/27/49	Wrong-Number Ringer Started Cleric On Phone Talks
2/9/49	Flashbulbs Latest Weapon in Fight On Selfish Seat-Savers at Concert
Feb. 1949	Only Chevrolet and Pontiac Dealers Cannot Deliver New Cars Immediately
July, 1949	Housing Count By Landlords, Federal Aides (first byline)
7/1/49	Clement Made Legion Leader; Was Unopposed
7/12/49	Red Bank, East Ridge to Seek Relief From 15-Cent Bus Fare in Chancery
7/14/49	Fight Is Planned By Tenant Group
7/14/49	Red Bank Drivers Offer Free Rides
7/14/49	Negro Drivers Jam Street In Hauling 440 To Registrars
7/19/49	Water Impounded By Dams Greatest in TVA History
7/19/49	Tennessee Visited By Fossil Hunters
7/20/49	Tenants to Show Picture Evidence
7/21/49	City To Welcome Legion's Throngs
7/22/49	Speaker Stresses Need of Histories
7/23/49	40-And-8 Greeted In State Reunion
7/24/49	Legionnaires, 8,000 Strong, Open Meeting
7/26/49	Strength Seen Without 'Bust' By Symington
7/30/49	2 Latvians Happy; Find U.S. Relative
7/31/49	Brainerd Kiwanis Is Host to 2,500"

8/21/49	County's Dogs 'Free' August 29
8/22/49	GI's Dividends In County Set At 2 Millions
8/27/49	States T-H Limits Prove New Unions
8/30/49	Vets Rush To Get Insurance Refund
8/31/49	Public Housing Delay Is Given City Realtors
9/5/49	Clinic in Mental, Emotional Problem, Now 2 Years Old, Treats 50 Clients
9/14/49	Frazier Maintains Hope for Hospital
9/20/49	Lookout Klan Starts Again
9/20/49	Hornbostels Seek Patients Release
9/27/49	Water System Seen on Signal
9/29/49	Advance Reported In Care of Ulcers
10/1/49	Lovell Field Men Saw Plane Crash
10/4/49	La Follette Urges Return to Ideals
10/16/49	TVA's 20-Cent Map A Popular Seller
11/2/49	Tropical Creatures at City's Zoo Are Now Bedded Down for Winter
11/5/49	Sewanee Installs Dr. Green As Its 10th Vice Chancellor
11/10/49	Your Coffee Cup Will Cost More
11/11/49	Norman Scott, in Leading Opera Role, Pleased With City, and Its Musicians
11/16/49	Campaigns Start on YDC Presidency
11/23/49	Knight of Knothole Is Col. Ochs; Prizes Given To Top-Notch Teams
Nov. 1949	City's Tots Have Biggest Christmas Of Lives in Store, Survey Indicates
Nov. 1949	Hens Dominate City's Tables; Warmer Today
Nov. 1949	Happy Crowd of 25,000 Watches Christmas Parade
Dec. 1949	Britons Find View of TVA Valuable
Dec. 1949	Tribute Paid to 110 Gray Ladies For 10 Years of Service to Sick
12/9/49	Train Delays Talk by Kiwanis Leader
12/16/49	McLellan's Head Optimistic on '50
12/17/49	'Hansel, Gretel' Is Well Received
12/18/49	Shoplifters, Lost Women and Tots Keep Police Busy in Jammed Stores
12/22/49	Boots, Maltese Dog, Ripe Old 22, Equivalent of 140 Among Humans
12/23/49	NC&St.L Telegrapher Soon Retires After Being With Company 55 Years
12/29/49	Lake Level Normal; Harbor Can't Take Drop of 2 Feet
1/8/50	Teacher Discovers Flag of City At Times; May Be Only One Left
1/16/50	Stapp, at 82, Still Runs Book Store; He Was Once Customs Agent Here
1/17/50	GI's Dividends Begin to Roll
1/18/50	TVA Impounds Flood Waters
1/20/50	Confederate Sons Told Of Memories

1/21/50	Indians' Removal Unfair, Says Corn
1/24/50	200 Veterans' Insurance Checks Due Every Day Here; High Digit Now 120
1/25/50	GI Insurance Refund Money's Effect May Be Overestimated, Check Shows
1/27/50	Blind Man Says State Trying to Close His Stand; He Wishes No Supervision
1/31/50	Blind Attack State Policy
2/2/50	Dog Waits Patiently for Mistress, Waitress, Outside Restaurant Daily
2/2/50	Blind Operator Given His Choice
2/4/50	Order New Study In Thrower Case
2/7/50	Blind Man's Case Given Washington
2/8/50	Patience Is Urged In Russian Deals
Feb. 1950	4&1/2 Miles of Pipe Used for Ice Rink
2/14/50	Tito Loan Awaits Expert On Mining
2/15/50	Creative Project Historians' Goal
2/16/50	Candidates Speak At Labor Meeting
2/18/50	Clements Takes St. Paul's Parish
2/22/50	Memorial Plaque Is Unveiled Today
2/23/50	Schoolfield and Hargraves in Tilt Over Support From Dillard's Ward
2/24/50	City High Student Is Radio Winner
2/26/50	Memphis' Ant Plague of 1925 Came, Disappeared in Mysterious Fashion
2/28/50	Delicate, Rugged Displays Industrial Show Contrasts
8/2/50	Changing Vote Officers Hit; Thrasher Attacks Primary
Feb. 1951	Council Ponders Wage Raise Issue
2/13/51	Klan Violence Used In Truancy in 1947; Charges Name Long
Mar. 1951	Joe N. Hunter, James Morgan May Be Judge
Mar. 1951	Judgeship Shades Commission Race
Mar. 1951	Little Sympathy Given Home Rule
Mar. 1951	Attorneys Await Naming of Judge
Mar. 1951	Warsaw Peace Congress Delegate Defends Red View, Finds Freedom
Mar. 1951	Election Dramas Always Are Hits
3/20/51	Testifies Man Kept Wife in Shack, Gave Her Children to His Mistress
3/22/51	Hamilton May Split Funds Despite Error, if Possible
3/23/51	10% Rise Goal For Teachers
3/25/51	Blind Association Cites John Spence
3/31/51	Schools' Union Address Topic
4/1/51	School Problem Puzzles Squires
4/5/51	Council Balks At Pay Raises; Session Fiery
4/8/51	Pay Issue Leads To Poor Morale

4/8/51	4 Opponents Loom For Frazier in '52
4/12/51	Clyde Baker Trial To Continue Today
4/13/51	Election Body Due for Shift
4/22/51	A Reporter Tells His Beat Good-Bye

The Memphis Press-Scimitar

11/28/51	City's Newest Housing Project
12/14/51	An $83 Million Idea is Born At LG&W
3/3/52	Our Negro Schools—25 in County Visited: 21 Found Lacking in Needed Facilities
3/4/52	Our Negro Schools—Six Are Far Below Standard
3/6/52	Our Negro Schools—Few Have Water or Lights
3/7/52	Our Negro Schools—In the Face of Inadequate Facilities
3/19/52	New Homes for 450 Families Will Rise Where Slums Now Stand in Disrepute
May, 1952	Bus Offer Rejected By Union
5/7/52	Threat of Bus Strike Hits Memphis
5/8/52	Bus Men Vote on Whether to Strike
5/9/52	Names Rejected By Union And Transit Co.
5/14/52	Union Calls Arbitrator
3/13/53	Folks Say Bob Crichton Used 'Steamroller' Like a Truck
4/13/53	Chandler & Cooper Both In Running to Head Convention
4/15/53	Our Delegates Ready to Tackle Revision Ideas Next Week
4/15/53	Legislative 'Basket Fishing' Problems Could Be Eliminated by Home Rule
4/16/53	What Goes On After the State Clock Stops
4/17/53	No One Opposes Raising Daily Pay of Legislators, Says Walter Chandler
4/20/53	Eyes of Tennessee Are on 99 at Nashville
4/20/538	From Shelby County Ready to Study Changes in State's Constitution
4/20/53	Not a Single Amendment in 83 Years
4/30/53	New Tax Boost For Property Owners
5/19/53	Underground Garage, a Rebuilt N. Parkway, Terminal Building
5/20/53	They Had Been Apparently Forgotten
7/24/53	Waring Calls For Talk On Improvement
8/8/53	In Fight to Make Living, Family Defends Against City
9/5/53	Ole Miss Is Sponsoring World Trade Institute
9/14/53	Cooper Points to Decline of Ag Exports
9/14/53	The Mid-South's Bread, Butter . . . And Cake
9/30/53	Sen. Hill Cites TVA's Benefits to Lower Mississippi Valley
10/10/53	Formal Discussion Set For the Near Future

9/18/64	Arrested Near His Wedding Day
9/30/64	Truancy Cases Bring Fines
10/28/64	Dutchman Likes Soviet Traders
11/5/64	Bulldozers to Aid Garbage Disposal
11/10/64	Memphis Will Get More of Sales Tax
11/18/64	Morris Has Named 375 Deputies
12/23/64	Shelby Stand For Speaker Not Clear
12/23/64	Garbage Dumps Target of Suits
12/23/64	Signs Bring Chuckles to Sheriff
12/23/64	Montsand West Hearing Jan. 8
12/23/64	Go-Go Club Would Be for Teen-Agers
12/23/64	Injured Farmer Still 'Serious'
12/24/64	Annex Study On For Whitehaven
12/30/64	Ewing On Job; Denies Guilt
12/31/64	Quit or Be Ousted Ultimatum to Ewing
1964?	Gore on Kerr-Mills: 'Bill Irresponsible'
1964?	3 to 1 Vote For Third, Madison
1/6/65	Ouster Suit Filed Against Jordan
1/7/65	MHA is Eyeing 300-Acre Area
1/11/65	Pay Hike For County Officials Requested
1/12/65	State's Help Asked On Health Centers
1/12/65	MHA Hears Pleas Against Project
1/15/65	More Assistance Sought for Prison School
1/21/65	Record CaseLoads For Shelby Courts
2/5/65	Not Cheerful, But Hopeful: Last Kefauver Book, on His Hearings
2/24/65	Editorial: Didn't Say 'Merge Building,' Says Lane—'But No Reason Not To'
2/25/65	23-Member Court Proposed (City Squires 14, County 9)
2/25/65	Editorial: Eight Years Ago Interest Was High In Schools Merger—Why Not Now?
2/26/65	Editorial: Since 1942, City and County Have Had Single Smooth-Working Health Unit
3/1/65	Chancery Jury Chosen In Jordan Ouster Case
3/2/65	Services, Favors To Jordan Told
3/3/65	Photostat of Jordan Check Is Ordered
3/5/65	Jordan Ouster Case Is Nearing Jury

* compiled by Suzanne McLain